剑桥双语分级阅读·小说馆（第2版）

原版系列编辑

The Amsterdam Connection

幕后黑手

[英] 休·莱瑟 著

王贵明 编译

北京语言大学出版社
BEIJING LANGUAGE AND CULTURE UNIVERSITY PRESS

CAMBRIDGE UNIVERSITY PRESS

社图号25014

图书在版编目（CIP）数据

幕后黑手 : 英汉对照 / (英) 休·莱瑟 (Sue Leather) 著; 王贵明编译. -- 2 版. -- 北京: 北京语言大学出版社, 2025. 3. -- (剑桥双语分级阅读小说馆). -- ISBN 978-7-5619-6733-1

Ⅰ. H319.4

中国国家版本馆CIP数据核字第2025RF5011号

幕后黑手
MUHOU HEISHOU

责任编辑：李　珍
责任印制：周　燚

出版发行：北京语言大学出版社
社　　址：北京市海淀区学院路 15 号，100083
网　　址：www.blcup.com
电子信箱：service@blcup.com
电　　话：编 辑 部 010-8230 1019
　　　　　发 行 部 010-8230 3650/3591/3648
　　　　　北语书店 010-8230 3653
　　　　　网购咨询 010-8230 3908
印　　刷：东港股份有限公司

版　　次：2017 年 6 月第 1 版　2025 年 3 月第 2 版
印　　次：2025 年 3 月第 1 次印刷
开　　本：880 毫米 × 1230 毫米　1/32
印　　张：5.875
字　　数：141 千字
定　　价：23.00 元

PRINTED IN CHINA

凡有印装质量问题，本社负责调换。售后QQ号1367565611，电话010-82303590

Preface

前言

“剑桥双语分级阅读·小说馆”是一套从剑桥大学出版社引进的面向非英语国家英语学习者的分级系列读物，由英语语言教学专家及小说作家合力创作。创作过程历时三十余年，出版后受到世界各地英语教师和英语学习者的喜爱，许多读本再版多次，三十余年来畅销不衰，成为受全球英语学习者青睐的优秀读本。

本系列读物具有以下突出特色：

1. 是原创英语读物，而非改编自普通作品的读物。因此，阅读本系列读物，我们读到的是原汁原味的原创英语，而非人为改编过的二手英语。

2. 是当代优秀短篇小说，而非年代久远的小说。因此，阅读本系列读物，我们读到的是当今鲜活的、学了就能用的英语，而非穿越时空的、学了用不上的英语；了解的是与读者同时代不同国家人们的生活和思想，而非隔代人的生活、文化和风土人情。

3. 是专为非英语国家的英语学习者量身定制的读物，而非为英语母语者所写的大众读物。因此，本系列读物是中国读者首选的英语学习读物。

4. 是英美知名小说家和英语语言教学专家合力创作的读物。小说家保障了读物的可读性与可欣赏性，英语语言教学专家保障了读物语言作为英语习得材料的科学性与可学性。本系列读物中的多个读本都曾在世界上颇具影响力的“语言学习者文学奖”(Language Learner Literature Award) 评选中获得大奖。因此，阅读本系列读物，我们会在欣赏小说的同时，自然而然地、有效地提高自己的英语水平。

5. 本系列读物的故事题材丰富多样，包括侦探、情感、历险、悬疑、人文、科幻、喜剧等，读者可以随心选择自己喜欢的类别阅读；故事内容生动有趣，故事情节引人入胜、扣人心弦，读者一旦开始阅读，就想一口气读完，使阅读真正升华到“悦读”。

6. 随书附赠的音频材料内容精彩，是专业配音员的演绎再创作。听着它，我们犹如在听广播剧、听评书，又仿佛是在听电影、听话剧……这种聆听英语的享受将彻底扫除学生对英语听力的畏难心理。

7. 本系列读物所使用的语言，既有英式英语，也有美式英语，对应的音频材料也相应分为英音和美音，读者可根据自己的喜好来选择。

8. 本系列近百本读物根据《欧洲语言共同参考框架》(CEFR) 和剑桥大学外语考评部开发的 ESOL 考试的标准来确定级别划分，是建立在科学研究和实践基础之上的分级。全套共分七个级别 (与中国学生英语基础水平的大致对应关系，请参见图书封底表格)，读者可根据自己的英语基础选择相应级别的读本来学习。

为了更好地帮助中国学生学习和欣赏，“剑桥双语分级阅读·小说馆”从剑桥大学出版社原版引进后又增加了以下内容：

1. 增加了适量的辅助学习内容，包括“读前思考”“读后活动”“学习指导”三个板块，其中“学习指导”板块又包括生词、短语和表达、文化点滴、阅读练习四项内容。增加这些板块的目的是全方位帮助学生提升英语阅读能力，扩充词汇量，扫除阅读中的文化障碍，增强对英语小说的鉴赏能力。

2. 增加了小说全文的参考译文。出于语言学习的考虑，译文多采用直译，但也尽量符合中文的表达习惯。

值得一提的是，所增加的辅助学习内容和参考译文，全部由来自全国不同省市知名中学（包括人大附中、北大附中、清华附中、黄冈中学、上海中学等三十余所中学）的一线英语教师完成。这些一线教师的加盟，确保了所加内容与中国学生的英语学习特点和学习需求相吻合，为学生阅读和欣赏读物、提高英语水平给予恰到好处的助力。

英语阅读是英语课堂的延伸和补充，也是培养英语语感、提高英语水平的有效途径。选择一套好的英语读物，收获的将不仅仅是语言的进步。欢迎年轻朋友们来到“剑桥双语分级阅读·小说馆”，打开一本本好书，品味一个个好故事，为实现梦想搭建桥梁。

北京语言大学出版社

Contents 目录

People in the story

故事中的人物

Kate Jensen: a news reporter on the *Daily Echo* in London

凯特·詹森：伦敦《每日回声报》的一名新闻记者

Rick: Kate's friend, also a news reporter

里克：凯特的朋友，也是一名新闻记者

Dave Balzano: the editor of the *Daily Echo*

戴夫·巴尔扎诺：《每日回声报》的主编

Elly van Praagh: a policewoman in the Amsterdam police and Kate's friend

埃莉·范普拉格：阿姆斯特丹警察局的一名女警察，凯特的朋友

Max Carson: Kate's friend and ex-boss

马克斯·卡森：凯特的朋友，前上司

Tom Carson: Max's brother, owner of Rotterdam City Football Club

汤姆·卡森：马克斯的弟弟，鹿特丹城市足球俱乐部的老板

Martijn Christiaans: a Dutch businessman

马丁·克里斯蒂亚安斯：一名荷兰商人

Jos van Essen: a retired footballer

乔斯·范埃森：一名退役的足球运动员

Raúl Sanchez: goalkeeper at Rotterdam City Football Club

劳尔·桑切斯：鹿特丹城市足球俱乐部的守门员

Joop de Vries: an inspector in the Amsterdam police

乔普·德弗里斯：阿姆斯特丹警察局的一名督察

Bert: a criminal

伯特：一名罪犯

Before reading

读前思考

1. How much do you know about the city Amsterdam and the country Holland?

2. Match the chapter titles with the sentences from each chapter.

Chapter 1 At the pub ______
Chapter 2 The past ______
Chapter 3 Amsterdam spring ______
Chapter 4 Talk with a striker ______
Chapter 5 Dinner at Sluizer's ______

a) It was a fine spring day; the sky was blue with little white clouds here and there.
b) Max looked at his watch and finished his beer quickly.
c) I remembered that I'd recently read in the newspaper that he'd retired from football.
d) We sat down and ordered steaks and a bottle of Bordeaux.
e) 'I was really young and really stupid, I guess. I wanted to write a big story.'

3. If you have the recording, listen to Chapter 1.

Chapter 1
At the pub

'You need a holiday, Kate,' said Max Carson. It was early evening and we were having a beer in the Queen's Head. 'A break from London,' he added.

'Oh sure, Max.' I smiled. 'Go and tell Balzano. I'm sure he'll agree with you!'

Dave Balzano was an excellent newspaper editor, but he was often angry with his reporters. In fact, he was famous for his bad temper. The thought of Balzano giving me a holiday because I needed one was funny. I said this to Max.

'So Dave hasn't changed, then?' asked Max, laughing. Max knew Dave – and me – from some years ago when we all worked on the *Manchester Evening News*. Max was the editor and Dave was head of foreign news. Max gave me my first job. I was just a young reporter then, trying to make a name for myself. That was before I came to London.

'Er ... no,' I said. 'He certainly hasn't.' I smiled and drank some of my beer. 'But tell me about you,' I added.

I hadn't seen much of Max for a while, mainly because he lived in Holland now. He had been born there. His mother was Dutch, his father was English. He came to England when he was in his early twenties to train as a journalist and he stayed. But Max retired from the *Evening News* five years ago when he was fifty-five, and returned to Holland.

'I'm fine,' said Max.

'And the club?' I asked.

Max's brother, Tom, was the owner and manager of Rotterdam City Football Club and the Carson Football School. When Max left the *Manchester Evening News* he had joined his brother, to help him with his business. Max now had about twenty-five per cent of the shares and a nice income for his 'retirement'.

'It's OK,' said Max.

'Only OK?' I asked, surprised.

'Mmm ... yes,' said Max. I got the feeling that he didn't really want to talk about it, so we changed the subject.

Max didn't often come to England these days, except to see friends and to look for new players for Rotterdam City Football Club. When he did come to

London he would come to the *Echo*'s offices to see me and we usually had a beer at the Queen's Head. It was a typical central London pub, full of office workers with mobile phones. It was smoky and noisy at this time in the evening, but the beer was good.

'So what's happening here in London, Kate?' Max asked.

Max always asked me about my latest story; he liked to know what was happening. He still loved the newspaper business. He and Balzano were complete opposites, and not just because Balzano's father was Italian and Max's mother was Dutch. Balzano was a very good editor, but you never knew when he was going to explode. Max, though, was calm and easy to work with – he was one of the best.

I told him about my last story and the reason I was so exhausted.

'You just need a break,' Max said again.

Max was right. I did need a holiday. Life in the city had been really tough for the past few months. I had had some difficult murder stories, the usual zero information from the London police and Balzano pushing me as usual. I was beginning to feel tired and the idea of getting away from London was a very attractive one.

'You like Holland, don't you?' asked Max suddenly.

I laughed. 'Well, yes, but ...' I'd been to Amsterdam once, chasing a story, and I'd loved it.

'And you know something about sport,' he added.

'Well, I know about karate and a bit about boxing,' I said. 'I don't know that much about other sports.' I had trained in karate for ten years and my father had been a boxer when he was young.

I looked at Max, waiting for the rest.

'Listen,' he said, 'why don't you come and write a story about our club in Holland?'

Rotterdam City Football Club was one of the top clubs in Europe now. Many of the young men who had been trained at the school – the Carson Football School – played for Rotterdam City. The club took kids who could play football off the streets and trained them to be the best. Football schools like theirs were one reason why Holland had so many great footballers. It was perfect: the school and the club.

Max had always been crazy about football. When he was editor of the *Evening News* he spent all his free time watching football matches. He even took me to see Manchester United once. He was one of those guys who knew the name of every footballer in Europe.

'What, me?' I laughed. 'A sports reporter? You know me, Max, I only write about crime.'

Max smiled. 'I know, Kate, and you're great. But it would be a holiday for you!'

Max looked at his watch and finished his beer quickly. He had arranged to have dinner with a friend that evening and he had to leave immediately. He was already late. He got up, promising that he would ring me in a few days.

But Max never rang. In fact, I never saw him again. Two days later, he was found lying dead in an Amsterdam street with twenty knife wounds in his body.

Chapter 2 The past

'Why did it happen, Rick?' I asked my colleague over and over again. 'It makes no sense. No sense at all!'

Rick and I were both news reporters on the *Daily Echo.* Our desks sat side by side. We worked together every day and at times like this Rick was the person I usually talked to. We'd heard the news of Max's death from the police in London.

'It was probably just a mugger, Kate, trying to get Max's money,' said Rick gently.

'What, in Amsterdam?' I said.

Amsterdam is one of the safest cities in the world. Soft drugs and sex, yes, but not much crime at all, certainly not violent crime. I had got to know the city quite well about two years before during a story about a British guy who was selling stolen paintings there. At that time I'd made a friend in the Dutch police.

Max had been found by the police in an area of Amsterdam called de Pijp in the early hours of the morning. I knew the Dutch police thought it was a mugging that had gone wrong – a drunk or a drug addict who tried to steal Max's money. It looked as if Max had fought back, but unfortunately the guy had a knife and had gone crazy.

'But what was Max doing walking around in the middle of the night?' I asked. 'And in Amsterdam – he didn't live in Amsterdam.'

Rick turned away from his computer screen and looked me straight in the eyes.

'Well, you know, Kate ... men in Amsterdam ...' he started. He didn't have to continue.

Amsterdam is the sex capital of Europe; everyone knows that. But I couldn't imagine Max visiting the famous red-light district of Amsterdam. I didn't know why exactly, but somehow it just wasn't like him. Not the Max I knew.

'Max?' I said. 'I don't think so.'

I had to admit that Rick was right, though. Max could have been there for any reason. After all, he lived in Holland. And why should Max tell me what he was planning to do? It wasn't as if we saw each other that often. I wondered now if I had really known him at all.

I thought for a moment and then said, 'You know, Rick, there's something I've never told you about Max.'

'What's that?' asked Rick.

'He saved my life,' I said.

'Saved your life?' repeated Rick, turning round to give me his full attention.

'Yes,' I said. 'When I first started as a reporter on the *Manchester Evening News* they asked me to write stories about babies and marriages. You know, the usual sort of thing ...'

Rick smiled and nodded. He knew exactly what I meant. His first job had been in a small town in Scotland where he spent two years writing about sheep stealing.

'But I really wanted to write about crime,' I continued. 'You know ... I was really young and really stupid, I guess. I wanted to write a big story – the biggest. I was hoping to make a name for myself by catching a really big fish.'

'Well, that's natural,' said Rick.

'Yeah, the problem was that the big fish was Johnny McGraw, one of Manchester's most dangerous criminals. He was really bad news, the kind of guy who would put people in the river with weights tied around their feet.'

'So what happened?' asked Rick.

'Max gave me this easy story, a break-in at a house in the centre of Manchester. The guy who lived in the house had tried to stop the gang from stealing his things. There was a fight and the man died of his wounds, so it became a murder. There were witnesses, people who saw it happen, but nobody could make them talk about it. Not even the police.'

I took a drink of my coffee. 'Anyway,' I continued, 'the guys were part of Johnny McGraw's gang and McGraw would kill anyone who talked.'

'And you tried to get them to talk?' asked Rick.

'You guessed it,' I said. 'It was my chance to get a really big story! But Johnny McGraw knew that it would lead back to him. He put a contract on my head for £25,000. If anyone killed me, McGraw would give them that amount of money.'

'So then what happened?' asked Rick, his eyes wide.

'Well, you can imagine that a lot of people were trying to kill me. I had to have police protection for a while,' I said. 'My own policemen twenty-four hours a day. I mean it was really serious. Then time went by and nothing happened. After about a month I came out of hiding and everything seemed fine. But then McGraw's men caught me.'

'But you got free?' Rick asked.

'Yes, with Max's help. Max knew where I was going that evening. When I disappeared he went out to look for me. He put his own life in danger for me. Finally, he came to an arrangement with McGraw and McGraw let me go,' I said.

I stopped. I wanted to cry but I couldn't.

'Anyway,' I continued, 'Max saved my life and I've never forgotten it.'

'Wow, Kate ... that's quite a story,' said Rick.

'Yeah,' I said. 'I've never told you, I guess because I was just so stupid. I hate to talk about how stupid I was,' I said.

Rick touched my arm and smiled.

But that was all in the past and now Max was dead. There were a number of people at the *Echo* who knew Max, and they all found his death hard to believe: it was so sudden and violent. For me the whole thing was worse because I'd seen him so recently. I knew that I had to go to Amsterdam, and I knew that if I wanted to go I had to ask my editor,

Dave Balzano.

* * *

'You want to go where, Jensen?' shouted Balzano. He was a fat sweaty man and he never spoke quietly.

'Amsterdam,' I said.

'Why do you want to do that?' asked Balzano angrily. 'Max was killed by a drug addict who was trying to get money!' Then he stopped for a moment. I could see that Balzano was sad at Max's death. After all, Max had been his editor too.

I looked at Balzano. 'I want to go, Dave,' I said quietly.

Balzano knew Max was special to me. He knew what had happened back in Manchester.

'OK, OK,' he said finally. 'Why don't you take Rick with you?'

'No, there's no need ... really,' I said. I wasn't sure what I would find out, if anything, but I knew I had to go. And I had to go alone. I caught the first plane I could. I was going to Amsterdam as Max had wanted – not to write about his club, but to find his killer.

Chapter 3 Amsterdam spring

I arrived in Amsterdam at 9:30 on Monday morning. I rang Elly van Praagh of the Dutch police from Schiphol Airport. Elly was the friend I had made during the case of the stolen paintings two years ago.

Elly wasn't working that morning and we arranged to meet two hours later at a café we knew in the Jordaan, an old part of Amsterdam. That would give me time to go to my hotel and check in. I caught the train from the airport and took a taxi into the centre from Central Station. The *Echo* had booked me into a hotel on the Keizersgracht. There were a lot of visitors in Amsterdam in spring and good rooms were difficult to find. The hotel wasn't very nice, but I didn't expect to be staying long. I left my bag and went to meet Elly.

Elly was already at the café when I arrived, sitting at a table outside, next to the Prinsengracht canal. She smiled and stood up as she saw me coming, and kissed me three times in the Dutch way. 'Hey, Kate, wonderful to see you,' she said.

Elly was typically Dutch, if there is such a thing. She was tall and very blonde, and looked like a sportswoman. In fact, she was a very good cyclist, and when she wasn't fighting crime in Amsterdam, was usually to be found cycling hundreds of kilometres around Holland with a number on her back. She looked like the daughter of a Dutch farmer, which she was, with red cheeks and bright blue eyes. And like most Dutch people of her age – she was in her early thirties – she spoke English very well.

We sat down and ordered coffee. It was a fine spring day; the sky was blue with little white clouds here and there.

'I'm sorry about your friend,' Elly said.

'Yes,' I said, staring at the red and white tablecloth. 'It's really sad.'

I told her about my meeting with Max just a few days ago. 'He seemed to be happy and said the club was doing OK,' I added.

Elly wasn't a football fan and knew nothing about the Rotterdam club. She did know about crime in Amsterdam though.

De Pijp, where Max had died, was one of the oldest parts of the city, a lively place with a wonderful street market at its centre, on a street called Albert Cuypstraat. Last time I was in Amsterdam I had gone shopping there for Dutch cheese and tulips to take home. It was strange to think that this lovely colourful place was where Max had lost his life.

'De Pijp is getting quite dangerous these days, Kate,' Elly said. 'There have been quite a number of stabbings and shootings. We've been busy down there.'

'So, it just looks like it was a mugging that went wrong?' I asked.

The waiter arrived with the coffees, Elly's black and mine *koffe verkeerd* or 'wrong coffee', the Dutch name for coffee with milk. Elly had ordered a cake too. All that crime-fighting and cycling made her hungry.

'Mmm,' said Elly, drinking some of her strong black coffee. 'I'm afraid that's what it looks like, Kate. He was just in the wrong place at the wrong time. Poor guy,' she added. 'Of course, there will have to be a postmortem.'

The police always asked for the examination of a

body found like this. I thought of Max lying dead with twenty knife wounds in his body. I felt cold, although the spring air was warm.

'So who found him?' I asked.

'We did. Well, one of the police teams going round the city late Thursday night,' Elly replied.

Thursday. Just two days after I had met Max at the Queen's Head. I looked out over the canal. It was a lovely warm day and the streets and bridges over the canals were full of people on bikes or on foot. It was beautiful. It was hard to think that Max was dead, and even harder to imagine that he had died in Amsterdam. It was such a lovely city.

'He was staying at the Tulip Inn on Spuistraat,' said Elly.

I didn't know the hotel, but I knew that Spuistraat was right in the old centre of the city.

'They didn't find much on his body at all. Just the usual,' she said.

Just the usual. In death people were almost the same. Some money perhaps, a few business cards, perhaps some photographs of the family. Except Max didn't have much family: his wife had died years ago and they didn't have any children. There was just his brother, Tom.

'Did the killer take his money, then?' I asked. If it was a mugging, surely the only reason could be money.

'Well, the police couldn't find his wallet,' she said.

Of course, that meant nothing, I thought. If someone wanted to make it look like a mugging, the first thing they would do was take money.

'We think that he probably fought back and his attacker went mad. It happens,' said Elly.

It certainly did.

'Why did he stay the night?' I asked. 'Why didn't he just go back to The Hague? It's only forty minutes or so on the train.'

I knew that Max lived near The Hague. He had asked me to stay at his house a few times, although I never had. I never seemed to have time. Now I would never have the chance.

'He must have had a business meeting the next morning. Apparently he often stayed in Amsterdam,' Elly said. 'The hotel manager said he'd stayed at that hotel before.'

Elly got up to go to work.

'Who's in charge of Max's case?' I asked.

'Joop de Vries, Murder Squad,' she said. Her face told me that she didn't like him much. 'Oh yes,' she added as she unlocked her bike and got on it. 'There was a card with a name and address in Max's pocket. I took a note of it.' She put her hand in her jacket pocket and brought out a piece of paper with something written on it. She gave it to me. It said: 'Jos van Essen, Oude Schans 141.'

I didn't know much about football, but I knew that name. Jos van Essen was one of the greatest footballers of all time.

Chapter 4 Talk with a striker

I watched Elly cycle off over the bridge, her blue jacket blowing out behind her.

I sat back down at the table and thought. Jos van Essen was a great footballer, like Pelé, Cruyff or Shearer. A real star. He had played for Holland lots of times as a striker and always scored lots of goals. He was also very good-looking. There were always reports in the newspapers about his girlfriends, who were usually models or actresses. I remembered that I'd recently read in the newspaper that he'd retired from football. People had been surprised because he was only twenty-eight, still quite young to retire.

I took out my map. Oude Schans was a long walk away. I had been there last time I was in Amsterdam, when I went to the Bimhuis jazz club. It was a very nice part of the city. It was a lovely day so I decided to walk, and do some thinking as I went. I walked off towards Oude Schans to see the ex-footballer.

There was a light wind and a smell of salt as I

crossed the canal. The sea was never far away in Amsterdam. I turned onto Raadhuistraat and walked towards Dam Square. So it looked as if Max had come to Amsterdam on business. I felt happy that Rick had been wrong about him coming for sex. That would mean that Max had been lonely and I didn't want to think of him as a lonely old man.

The retired footballer lived in an apartment beside the canal, Oude Schans, in one of the oldest parts of Amsterdam. It was 1:30 when I got to his apartment block. I pressed the bell and Jos van Essen's voice came through the intercom. I told him I was a friend of Max's and the door opened.

'Come up to the top floor, Miss Jensen,' he said. His voice was soft and pleasant.

Like all Dutch houses, this one was tall and thin, and the stairs were very narrow. I finally got to the top and knocked. I heard the sound of van Essen unlocking his door. It took some time – there were three or four locks. Then there he was, smiling. He had a beautiful smile.

'It's quite a climb, isn't it?' he said. He looked just like the pictures I'd seen of him on the *Echo*'s sports pages. He was tall, with the most beautiful dark brown eyes and the whitest teeth I'd ever seen.

He was wearing black jeans and a pink shirt, which looked great against his black skin. His body still looked fit. And what a body! I was beginning to like my work.

'Come in, Miss Jensen,' he said, still smiling. He held open the door and showed me into his apartment.

The apartment was not very big, but apartments in Holland are usually quite small. He must have been very rich, though – the furniture looked expensive. I remembered reading something in a newspaper about him when he was still playing for Rotterdam. The newspaper story had said that he was earning millions. I supposed that this was just his city apartment. He would have a big house somewhere, perhaps at the beach. Perhaps abroad.

Although the apartment was small, it was in a great position. It looked right onto the canal, and the house where Rembrandt had lived was nearby. The large French windows were open and I could feel the warm air coming into the room. The only sign that the apartment was owned by a footballer was the photograph on the coffee table of the Rotterdam City team which had won the European Cup four years ago. Jos was in the front row. Max and a man who looked like him but younger – Tom I guessed – were standing beside the team smiling.

'Ah, yes, the good times!' he said, seeing me look at the photo. 'When we were the best!' Jos looked a little sad.

He offered me a comfortable armchair, then said, 'Have some coffee, Miss Jensen. I have a fresh pot ready.' He went into the kitchen and returned almost immediately with the coffee.

'So, you're a sports reporter, writing about Rotterdam City?' he asked as he put the coffee pot on the low glass table.

'Yes, I'd like to write about the club,' I said. 'I think football fans in England would find it interesting.'

I explained that I'd seen Max just two days before he died.

'You're a friend of Max's?' he said, pouring me a cup of coffee. 'It's just so sad, awful ... What a terrible thing to happen. I can hardly believe it.'

Jos van Essen looked like he was going to cry, but he managed to stop himself.

'Yes, it's terrible,' I said, 'and so senseless. The police think he was killed by a mugger.'

'Yes,' said Jos in a worried voice. 'That's what they

think ...'

For a moment I thought he was going to say more, but he decided not to.

'You knew Max well then?' I continued.

'Oh yes. I knew him very well. He really helped me when he came to the club. Really helped me to become a great footballer.'

He reached for his coffee cup. Again I thought he was trying not to cry. Then he went on.

'Rotterdam City Football Club was good to me,' he said, looking at the photo again. 'I was a ten-year-old kid in a children's home when Tom Carson found me. You know the story, it's famous. Tom came along and watched me play. He saw something, something that no-one else could see. He took me to the Carson School, gave me a good education, fed me, let me play football. At the school they trained me how to really play ... They gave me football boots for the first time.'

He smiled. 'I still have my first pair of football boots,' he continued. 'Before that I'd only played in old trainers. They gave me the opportunity to be really good. And for the first time in my life I was happy.'

Jos looked at me and took a deep breath.

'And then Max really helped me to be the best,'

he said. 'When he came to the club I was a good footballer. But Max talked to me, helped me, gave me what I needed to play for Holland, to become great ... and he was great, a great man.'

Jos van Essen had played for Holland and had been in the team that had won the World Cup.

'I don't really understand what Max's job was at the club,' I said. 'Isn't Tom the coach, the manager?'

'Yes, that's right,' said Jos. 'Max was a scout. He helped Tom by travelling around Holland and the rest of Europe, looking for good young players for the club and kids for the school.'

'And it seems he was good at it,' I said.

'The best,' said Jos.

Max had always been very active and even after he'd retired, he still loved to travel and to work. I also remembered that Max had always known when a young football player was going to be great.

'Were Max and his brother close? Did they have a good relationship?' I asked.

Jos looked a little uncomfortable. 'Yes ...' he answered slowly. 'Although they've been arguing lately.'

'What about?'

'I don't know,' Jos said and looked away. I had a feeling he knew more than he would say.

'Why did Max have your card on him when he was found?' I asked. If Jos and Max knew each other so well, why did he need a visiting card?

'I've just moved here. It's my new apartment,' explained van Essen, smiling and waving his hand around the room. 'I saw Max on Thursday evening and gave him my new address, that's all.'

'You saw him on Thursday?' I asked.

That was the evening Max was found dead in de Pijp.

'Yes,' he said. 'I told the police. Thursday evening, early, about seven. We had a drink together at De Beiaard bar on Herengracht. We often met there when we were both in town, just for a chat and a beer.' He smiled and added, 'They have a great choice of beer.'

'And then?' I asked.

'I don't know what he did exactly,' said Jos. 'I had a dinner date and he said he had to visit someone.'

'Did he say who?' I asked.

'No.'

'Was he walking?' I asked.

'No. He said he was going to get a taxi,' Jos answered.

'So, the person he was visiting didn't live in the centre,' I said.

'I'm not sure,' said Jos. 'Max often took taxis even short distances. He didn't like to get too tired because of his heart.'

'His heart?' I asked.

'Yeah, Max had a bad heart. He had a heart attack ... oh, about four years ago I think,' said Jos.

That was something I didn't know about Max.

'And he took pills?'

'Yeah, I think so ... Yes, I'm sure. I've seen him take them quite a few times,' Jos replied.

'Max told me that there were some problems at the club,' I lied.

Jos looked surprised.

'Er ... well, yes. I don't know. I don't really know anything about it. I left about a year ago,' he said. 'I don't know what's going on now.' He looked away from me.

'You didn't talk about it?' I asked.

'No, we didn't,' said Jos. He said it in a way that made it sound like there was nothing more to say.

'And what about your retirement from football? Why are you retiring at only twenty-eight?' I asked. 'It's very young.'

'Oh, you know, I want to do other things,' he said, still looking away. 'I'm not sure what yet, but something different. I'm still young but I've been playing football for a long time, Miss Jensen.'

I drank my coffee and got up to go.

'I'm staying at the Continental on Keizersgracht,' I said as I was leaving.

Jos van Essen unlocked the four locks on his door and said goodbye.

Chapter 5
Dinner at Sluizer's

An hour after ringing van Essen's doorbell I was back on Oude Schans, looking at the boats on the canal and watching the light dancing on the water.

I looked at my map and wondered what to do. Perhaps I'd go to de Pijp, the area of the city where Max's body had been found.

De Pijp was at the other end of Amsterdam so I walked a little in the warm sunshine, then took the tram. When I got there I walked around the streets for a while and through the market. It was an interesting colourful place. You could buy anything there: fresh fruit and vegetables, meat, eggs, cheese and flowers. Holland was famous for its tulips of course, and the tulips here were lovely.

I passed by the narrow street where Elly told me they had found Max. At one end of it was a bigger street; at the other end was a park called Sarphatipark. It was this area around the park that was becoming more and more dangerous, Elly had said. There was only one apartment block on one side of the street. Even in the sunshine, it looked sad and grey.

The police had put a rope around the area where Max had died to stop people going near it. I felt cold as I looked at it. I went into a small café-bar on one corner of the market, sat at the bar and ordered tea to warm myself up.

There were only a few customers in the bar, mostly men who looked like they worked on the market. The bar owner was a friendly guy with a big stomach and a red face. He started talking to me. His English was quite good. We chatted about this and that, and then I said, 'I heard there was a murder here the other night.'

'Oh yes,' said the barman. 'Big trouble. We've had the police here almost all the time.'

'Does it happen a lot around here?' I asked.

'Well, it's getting worse,' he said.

'It's terrible what's happening to this area,' said a voice at my side.

I turned round. Next to me was an old guy drinking jenever, the strong Dutch gin, and smoking a cigarette. He was short and his skin was dark, like he had worked outside all of his life. He had very little hair and when he smiled at me I noticed that he had just a few dark brown teeth.

'I'm Bert,' he said, holding out his hand.

Bert liked to talk. He asked me where I was from and we talked about London, which he had visited twenty years before. We chatted for a while, then returned to the murder.

'Everybody round here heard about it,' he said. 'It happened just two streets away.' He took a drink of his jenever. 'Yes, the place was full of police for days.' Bert's face looked sad. 'It's terrible ... terrible.' I wondered whether it was the violent crime or having the police around so much in de Pijp that Bert thought was so terrible.

We talked some more as I drank my tea and then I got up to go. 'If you hear anything about what happened, give me a call. I'm a friend of the dead guy's family,' I lied. I gave Bert a piece of paper with the telephone number and the name of my hotel. He was staring at the paper as I left the bar.

I went back to the hotel. In my room I lay down on the bed. I had a few questions in my head: Why had Max wanted me to write about the club so much? Was it just that he thought I needed a holiday? And why was Jos van Essen so frightened? I put a John Coltrane cassette in my walkman and listened to some of the best jazz saxophone music the world has ever known.

I woke up to the sound of the phone on my bedside table ringing in my ears. It took me a second to realise that I'd been asleep, another to remember where I was. I still had my headphones on my ears, although the cassette had stopped. I shook myself awake and took the headphones off. It was Elly.

'Uh ... Elly, what's up?' I was still stupid with sleep and had no idea what time it was. It was dark, though.

'Kate, are you asleep?' she asked.

'Well, I was. What time is it?' I asked, waking up a little.

'It's seven o'clock and I've just finished work. Kate, let's meet for a drink,' she said.

Half an hour later we were in a bar near the hotel having a beer. I told Elly about my meeting with van Essen and my visit to de Pijp.

'You're lucky!' she said and smiled. 'Most women would kill for the chance of talking to van Essen.'

'Well, most of the time I'm interviewing ugly criminals.' I laughed. 'It was great to have someone attractive to talk to!'

'Did you get anything interesting?' she asked.

'Not much,' I said. 'But I got the feeling that he's frightened of something ... or somebody. His apartment was locked up like a bank!'

Elly laughed.

'I'm just going to ring Balzano,' I said, moving towards the telephone at the other end of the bar. I didn't have much to tell him, but it was always a good idea to keep him calm.

'No, wait,' she said and held onto my arm. 'Wait until after dinner. I've got something to tell you.'

We chose Sluizer's restaurant on Utrechtsestraat for dinner and took a taxi there. It was one of my favourite Amsterdam restaurants. It was really two restaurants, the fish restaurant and the meat restaurant, and they were both wonderful. There were beautiful old mirrors everywhere and waiters in black suits and white aprons. And the food was always great; it didn't matter which part you chose. Tonight we chose the meat restaurant. We sat down and ordered steaks and a bottle of Bordeaux. It had been a busy day and I was very hungry.

Suddenly Elly looked at me in that special way she did when she had something important to say. I could see her serious face in the large mirror next to the table. 'Kate, there's something I need to tell you,' she said.

'Mmm?' I said, chewing a piece of steak.

'They think they found Max's killer today,' she said.

I put my knife and fork down. 'They?' I asked.

'De Vries's men. They picked someone up. They're fairly sure he did it.'

'But has this guy confessed – said that he did it?' I asked.

'No,' she said. 'I don't think so, but they found Max's wallet in his apartment. They're looking for the knife now.'

'Who is it?' I asked.

'A guy who lives in the area,' she said. 'A well-known local drug addict and mugger.'

So that was it, I thought. It looked like everyone was right. Max's murder had been a senseless killing by a sick guy who needed money for drugs. I put my head in my hands – I felt ill.

'I'm sorry, Kate,' Elly added.

I couldn't speak for a moment. Then, suddenly, the memory of Max talking to me at the Queen's Head that night came back to me. 'You need a holiday,' he had said. 'Come and write about the club.' Why exactly did Max want me to write about Rotterdam City?

'I don't believe it,' I said, looking up. The words

were a surprise, even to me.

I guessed that the Amsterdam police wanted to catch the killer quickly. And it would be easier for them if the killer was a local criminal who was annoying them. They were just like police everywhere.

'But Kate ...' started Elly.

'I don't know why, but there's something about this that isn't right,' I almost shouted. The middle-aged couple sitting near us looked towards me. I was sweating, and I still felt sick. I spoke more quietly. 'There's something else ...'

Elly smiled kindly at me. 'Look, Kate, I'm just telling you. I'm not even working on the murder.' I knew that was true. Elly was working on another crime on the other side of the city.

'I know, Elly, and thanks,' I said. 'But I just have a feeling ...'

She smiled again. 'I don't know what the truth is,' she continued, 'but I thought I'd better tell you. Tomorrow de Vries will tell the newspapers and TV and everyone in the world will know.'

I knew that Elly thought that my feelings for Max were so strong that I couldn't accept his death, couldn't accept the way he had died. I was beginning to wonder about it myself. It was hard when a guy had saved your life. It was hard to see things clearly. I wondered what Balzano would think.

Balzano! I suddenly remembered I had to phone him. I quickly drank half a glass of wine to make me brave, and ran to the phone in the hall.

'Jensen!' screamed Balzano. I held the phone away from my ear for a moment. Balzano was unhappy about something and when he was unhappy he never said hello.

'At last! I thought you'd disappeared,' he shouted. Disappeared! I'd only been in Amsterdam one day.

'Listen,' he continued, 'there's a story in the *Gazette* this evening about Max. By Joe Simmons.' Balzano said the name through his teeth. The *Gazette* was the other big newspaper in London, and Joe Simmons was their best reporter.

'What ... what's Simmons saying?' I asked.

'That they've found the guy who killed Max,' Balzano continued. 'That it's all over. What the hell are you doing there, running round Amsterdam ... What am I paying you for, Jensen?'

Even with the phone held away from my ear I could hear Balzano clearly.

This was bad news. Simmons had somehow got

the story first, and one thing that made Balzano really angry was when the *Gazette* got a story before us. Well, I wasn't happy about it either.

Balzano stopped for a few seconds to catch his breath and I jumped in.

'Dave, listen. It's not true ... at least I don't think it is,' I said, hoping I was right.

'Not true?' screamed Balzano. 'For God's sake, Jensen. They've found Max's wallet! The guy had his wallet! What more do you want?'

'I don't know Dave,' I said. 'I just have a feeling that there's something else. Give me time.'

I put the phone down.

'Well?' asked Elly, who had almost finished her steak by the time I returned. All that cycling certainly made her hungry.

'Bad news,' I said. 'The news is out already, true or not, and Balzano is not a happy man. He nearly had a heart attack when I said I needed time, but he agreed in the end.' Elly laughed. She had never met Balzano, but she understood.

Balzano had given me three days to find a story or leave Amsterdam. I pulled my steak, now getting cold, back towards me. I had a feeling that I was going to need all my strength.

Chapter 6
Bert's story

Back at the hotel there was a message from Bert, the old guy I'd met in the bar in de Pijp. He'd left a telephone number. It was late but I rang him from my room. Bert was still at the bar where I'd left him hours before – I could hear people talking behind him and the sound of glasses. I wondered if he spent all his time there.

'I have some information for you,' he said. 'Some really good information. But I need something.'

'Something?' I asked.

'Some money,' he whispered. 'Four hundred guilders.' Four hundred guilders. That was over a hundred pounds. It was a lot of money if the information was useless, but I had to say yes. Balzano was getting very impatient and I had nothing else.

'OK, Bert, that's fine,' I said. 'Can you come to the hotel now?'

Bert arrived at the hotel at 11:30, looking a lot more drunk than when I had left him. We went into the bar; he ordered jenever and I paid for it. I had put the four hundred guilders in an envelope and now I put it on the table, my hand covering it.

'Well, Bert,' I said. 'What is it?'

He looked around the room, as if he were expecting someone to be listening. Then he looked at the envelope and drank some of his jenever.

'I know someone,' he whispered. 'He saw what happened to your friend on Wednesday night. Says your friend was already dead when he was taken to that street. Someone took him out of a car, then knifed him many times. But he was already dead. He was dead before. He's sure of it.'

Bert looked at the envelope under my hand. I didn't move it. 'Why doesn't this person talk to the police?' I asked.

Bert laughed. 'Oh, he doesn't like the police, you know. He won't tell the police anything!' Well, that was possible. There were a lot of people who didn't like the police. Especially if they were criminals.

'And where was he, this person?' I asked.

'He was looking from an upstairs window,' said Bert. 'Something woke him up. He didn't turn the light on, just went to the window. He could see everything.'

I wondered whether Bert was telling the truth. It was more likely, I guessed, that this person was breaking into a house at the time and that was why he couldn't tell the police. I imagined that Bert had friends like that. Or was it even Bert himself?

'Was it a man or a woman with my friend?' I asked.

'Well, a man, my friend guesses, but it was dark,' said Bert.

'And the car, what kind of car was it?' I asked.

Bert thought. He didn't know. It was too dark and anyway it was parked down the other end of the street.

'I thought he could see everything,' I said.

'Well, you know, almost everything,' said Bert. 'He saw someone stabbing him with a knife, that's certain.'

'So what about the knife?' I asked. 'What happened to it?'

Bert just shook his head. 'Who knows?' he said.

'Look, Bert,' I said. 'I know the police have already picked up a guy. They say they found my friend's wallet in his apartment.'

'I know, I know,' said Bert impatiently. 'But it's not true. The guy they picked up – Cor Schaap – he couldn't kill anyone, everyone on the street knows that. He's never killed anyone before. Why should he start now?'

'There's always a first time,' I said.

'No, no,' said Bert. 'He just stole the wallet from the dead body. That's what everyone thinks ... Everyone except the police.'

Well, I thought, it was possible.

I gave Bert the envelope. He took it quickly, finished his drink and almost ran out of the door with the money. I had no idea whether the information he'd given me was true. Perhaps Bert had just seen the opportunity to make some easy money. It could be an expensive hundred pounds for me.

I went back to my room, lay on my bed, and looked at a report of Rotterdam Football Club's match against Leiden last night. It was from *Het Parool*, a Dutch newspaper. I couldn't read Dutch but I could see that Rotterdam had lost 2–0 to Leiden. Rotterdam had played very badly.

I wondered what Tom Carson, Manager of Rotterdam City FC, would have to say about that.

Chapter 7
Rotterdam

Amsterdam Central Station is a beautiful building, but I didn't have much time to look at it. My meeting with Tom Carson was at 10:00 on Tuesday morning at the Rotterdam City Football Club offices. It was almost 8:30 when I arrived at the station and bought a ticket, some coffee and a croissant, and got on the train.

Holland is such a small country that all the towns and cities are close to each other. It would take me just over an hour to get to Rotterdam, so I sat back in my seat and enjoyed the view. Flat green fields, flower farms and cows. And of course, water. In Holland there is water everywhere.

It was hard not to think about Max's death. Before leaving me the night before, Elly had warned me not to get too involved. But I was involved already. I had become involved when Max Carson had talked to me just a few days ago in the Queen's Head. I was involved because Max was dead. I was involved because he had saved my life: I owed him something.

As I looked out of the window at the Dutch

countryside, I thought about what I'd read last night about Rotterdam's match against Leiden. I didn't know much about football, but I knew you had to score goals to win. Tom Carson would not be happy, I guessed. But there were more important things than football – the guy had just lost his brother.

The train soon arrived at Rotterdam station. Rotterdam is very different from Amsterdam, and you see the differences as soon as you reach it by train. Rotterdam is just like any other modern city, with tall glass buildings and apartment blocks. It has none of the beauty of Amsterdam with its lovely old buildings and canals.

I met Tom Carson at the club offices. He was a slim grey-haired man of about fifty and he looked so much like Max that I suddenly felt sad. Tom had the body of a sportsman. He had played for Ajax when he was younger, and he still looked like he could kick a ball around a field.

'It's really good of you to see me,' I said. 'I'm so sorry about Max.'

'Yes, it's awful,' said Tom Carson. 'Hard to believe really. Just senseless.' Max's brother shook his head. He looked tired.

'Max was a wonderful man,' I said.

We talked about Max a little and our time together in Manchester. Then Tom Carson asked, 'What can I do for you, Miss Jensen?'

'Well, I want to write something about a Dutch football club, comparing it to an English club,' I explained. 'You know, training – that sort of thing. Rotterdam City seems like a good choice. But perhaps it's not a good time ...'

I didn't tell Carson that Max had wanted me to come and write a story about the club.

'No, it's fine,' he said. 'Life goes on. We have to think about the future of the club. The boys are going to start training in a few minutes.'

Although he was sad at his brother's death, Tom Carson did not want to miss the opportunity of some good publicity for his club. He was a good businessman, I thought.

We walked out to the training ground and sat at the side. The 'boys' started coming out from a dressing room under the offices.

'They're getting ready for a European Cup game right now. They play Barcelona here at home tomorrow evening,' he explained.

I wondered how they would play against Barcelona after their terrible match against Leiden. Barcelona were one of the best teams in Europe. If they couldn't win against Leiden, what hope did they have against 'Barça'?

'I think they'll be OK,' said Carson, as if reading my thoughts. But I had the feeling that he didn't really believe it.

The players were doing their warm-up exercises out on the field. The sun was shining and there was a light wind, as usual in Holland. We talked about the training and I watched the team a bit more, hoping that Carson wouldn't realise how little I knew about football.

'The interesting thing,' said Carson, 'is the school and the team – you know, having both. It makes us different.'

'Yes, it sounds interesting,' I said. 'I'd really like to visit the school if possible.'

Carson smiled. 'Well, that couldn't be easier, Miss Jensen. It's just down the road. I'll take you myself,' he said. Before leaving, I looked once more at the team on the field. The players were practising crossing the ball to the strikers, who then shot at goal. The strikers were strong and mostly managed to get the ball into the goal.

'They look good,' I said to Tom Carson. 'I guess you're hoping for a few goals tomorrow night.'

Carson gave a worried smile.

Tom Carson showed me round the Carson Football School. The boys lived at the school. They slept there, ate there, studied there and played football there. It was modern and clean, with very good teaching plus football training that Tom said was 'first class'. The boys were everywhere, studying and playing football. They were quite young, between eight and fifteen I guessed, though there were two or three older ones.

'A lot of them come from very poor families, Miss Jensen,' said Tom, as we watched a group of ten boys doing some practice. They were kicking the ball round some boxes that had been placed in a line, then getting to the end and shooting at the goal. They looked good, I thought. Good sportspeople are all the same in some ways. It doesn't matter whether they do karate, play tennis or play football. They have good balance and keep their heads very still.

'Some of the boys are Dutch, but some come from South America and Africa. We find young boys who are really good and bring them back here,' he continued.

'And that was what Max did?' I asked.

'Yes,' he said. 'Max looked for kids like these, and also good players in other teams.'

I took some notes for my 'story' and looked around a little more. The boys certainly looked happy and well cared for.

'And most of them become professional footballers?' I asked.

'Most of them,' he said. 'If they're good enough.'

Tom Carson and I left the school. I shook his hand, said goodbye and went back to Rotterdam station. On the train back to Amsterdam it was hard not to think about the manager's sad smile. Carson was unhappy, I thought, and not only because he'd just lost his brother.

Chapter 8
Life gets interesting

Back in Amsterdam, I went to the main public library – I had some detective work to do. It was time to find out exactly who had money in Rotterdam City Football Club. Max had told me that he had about twenty-five per cent of the shares in the club, but was the club owned just by the Carson brothers?

The library assistant showed me to a computer where I could get onto the Internet and I began work. I searched for information about Rotterdam City Football Club over the past five or six years. Two hours later, I was beginning to build up a picture of what had happened to the club.

It was interesting reading. Tom Carson's shares in the club had gone down from seventy-five per cent to just thirty per cent over the past two years. But Tom's shares hadn't gone to Max. Max's shares remained at twenty-five per cent during the whole time he was at the club. Most of the shares had gone to someone called Martijn Christiaans. I looked back over the past few years. Christiaans had started buying shares two years ago and had started with just ten per cent, but he now owned forty-five per cent of Rotterdam City Football Club.

Who was Martijn Christiaans, I wondered, and why was Tom Carson allowing him to buy up his club?

I wondered what had happened to Max's shares now. No doubt they had passed straight to Tom Carson. With Max dead, his brother now had fifty-five per cent of the club – a very strong position to be in.

I left the public library. It was time for a bit more detective work.

I started with the telephone book back in my hotel room. I was lucky. I found just one Martijn Christiaans in the book, with an address on Herengracht. I went to take a look.

Herengracht was just a five-minute walk away from the hotel. As I walked I thought of the story that I would tell Christiaans if he was at home. I was writing a story on old buildings in Amsterdam and I wanted to talk to him about his house. I knew that Herengracht was full of wonderful old houses. I arrived at number 141 and looked up at the top of the house as if I was suddenly interested in old buildings. It was beautiful. Probably 17th century, and in very good condition. Christiaans was obviously extremely rich.

I took a deep breath and went up the steps to the door. It was made of beautiful black wood and there was a silver bell above the name. I rang the bell, waited, then rang again. There was no-one at home.

Just as I was turning to go, a young woman of about twenty-five arrived at the next house, carrying shopping bags. She said something to me in Dutch, so I said, 'Sorry, I don't understand.'

'Oh, sorry,' said the woman, smiling at me. 'I said if you're looking for Mr Christiaans, I saw him going out early this morning.'

'Do you know what kind of work he does?' I asked.

'Mmm, I'm not really sure. I don't know him very well.' And with that she opened the door of her house and went inside.

It seemed I'd missed Christiaans, so I went back to the hotel. There I had better luck. There was a letter waiting for me at reception. It had been posted yesterday in the city and had arrived in the second post. The name and address on the envelope had been typed. It just said 'Miss Jensen', then the name and address of the hotel. I opened the envelope. Inside there was a short note, written by hand in capital letters:

DEAR MISS JENSEN

YOU SHOULD LOOK INTO THE MONEY THAT WAS BET ON LEIDEN TO WIN THE MATCH AGAINST ROTTERDAM

A FREIND

I didn't know who had written the letter, but it was someone who couldn't spell 'friend'.

'Good news?' asked the young woman at reception.

'Maybe ...' I said.

Who had bet on Leiden to win the match? Where could I find out? I rang Elly.

'Now, let's see,' said Elly. 'Most of the betting on sport is done through a betting office called Kanters. Try a guy called Ronnie in the office here in Amsterdam and give him my name. He owes me something. He should be able to help you.' Then she added, 'And be careful, Kate.'

A few minutes after talking to Elly, I rang Jos van Essen.

'Miss Jensen, what a surprise!' he said.

'Mr van Essen,' I said, 'I was wondering ... I've heard that Rotterdam are playing Barcelona tomorrow and, well, I'd like to see the match.' I knew that as an ex-player he would have tickets.

'Well ... yes, of course. Why not come with me?' he asked.

'That would be great!' I said.

'Good. I'll pick you up at your hotel around 5:30. The match starts at 7:30. Good night,' said the beautiful striker.

I put the phone down. Life, I thought, was beginning to look interesting.

* * *

That evening life suddenly got even more interesting. At about 10:30 I decided to go out for a walk. I needed some air and I needed to think. It was dark by now and there were very few people walking around near the hotel. I walked slowly down Keizersgracht, staring at the pavement, thinking about everything that had happened during the day. I walked down by the canal.

Suddenly a car stopped in the street next to me. A dark shape jumped out, came up behind me and pulled my arm behind my back. It hurt like hell. 'Get in the car and don't make a noise, or I'll break your arm,' the guy said. I didn't recognise the voice.

I raised my foot and kicked the guy hard in his

right leg. At the same time I pulled back my free arm and put my elbow into his chest. My attacker wasn't expecting this and it worked well, taking his breath away.

The guy let go and I turned round quickly. I looked up and saw a tall dark-haired man with clear blue eyes.

'Come here,' he said. He pulled me, trying to get me into the car.

'Hey, say please,' I said, fighting back. He was smiling, almost making fun of me. That made me really mad. He was quite strong, and much bigger than me, but my years of karate training had made me fast. I also knew how to surprise him.

He managed to pull me nearer to the car. I stepped back on my left foot, pulled up my right leg quickly and gave him a karate kick in the stomach, with my right foot. I put all my weight behind the kick and it surprised him. He was tall, but if you hit the stomach, size doesn't matter. He started to fall over like a tree and, as he fell, I hit him on the side of his head with my elbow. The elbow is the hardest bone in the body and in no time he was on his knees, holding his head between his hands. He realised then that it was not going to be as easy as he had thought. He hadn't

expected me to put up such a fight. He quickly climbed back into his car looking around nervously. He was probably afraid that the noise would bring people out to see what was happening.

He was going to get away. I looked around to see if there was anyone who could get help, but the street was empty. I wanted to stop him, but there was no way I could stop him on my own. The next moment there was a screeching noise as my attacker started his car, put his foot down hard, and raced off down the road.

Chapter 9
The Amsterdam Connection

I ran up the stairs to my room and locked the door behind me, breathing heavily. I guessed that this guy had been outside the hotel, watching me, waiting for his chance. I took a whisky from the mini-bar in my room and drank it quickly. I went to bed, but I slept badly.

The next day I planned to go to see Ronnie, Elly's 'friend' at Kanters. But before I could leave my hotel room, I got another surprise. Elly came to the hotel on her way to work. The Amsterdam police had got the results of Max's postmortem. A friend of hers in de Vries's team had told her about it.

'They're saying he definitely died of the knife wounds,' she said. 'He lost a lot of blood. And it's ninety-five per cent certain that he died there, in de Pijp.'

'And they still think it's this guy Schaap?' I asked.

'Yes,' she said. 'Although they haven't found the

knife.'

I told Elly what Bert had told me. Elly just looked at me. She didn't have to say anything. We both knew that it was more than possible that Bert was telling lies just to get money.

'What about the time of death?' I asked her.

'They're not completely sure, but it was somewhere between midnight and 3:30 in the morning,' said Elly.

I didn't tell Elly anything about what had happened the night before. She left to go to work and I left to go to Kanters. Outside the hotel I looked around me and then stopped a taxi. From now on I had to be careful.

At the Kanters office I asked to see Ronnie. A young woman led me into a back office where Ronnie sat working at a computer. He just carried on staring at the computer when I went in, hardly looking at me. The office was dark, with just a small window at the back. Ronnie was a thin little man of about forty, with almost no hair. His skin was white and he looked unhealthy. I guessed he spent most of his time working in this dark room. I explained what I wanted.

'I can't give you that type of information,' he said,

without looking up.

I said Elly's name. It worked. He turned round, looked me up and down, then closed the door so that no one from the front office could hear us. I don't know what he owed Elly, but it was obviously something big.

'Come back in an hour,' he said in a low voice.

I went out, bought a newspaper and went into a café. I looked at the sports pages. There was a report about tonight's match and I read what I could. I looked out of the window, drank my coffee and thought.

If Max had been knifed somewhere else, as Bert said, what about the blood? The blood would be in the car, everywhere. That meant a bloody car left somewhere, or a big clean-up.

I went back to see Ronnie, who by now had the information on his computer screen. I had told him that I was looking for a big bet, a large amount of money on Leiden to win the match against Rotterdam.

'Everybody expected Rotterdam to win,' said Ronnie. 'They were the favourites. Leiden were six to one. That means if you bet a guilder, you got six guilders,' he explained.

I smiled. 'Oh really?' I said. Sometimes it was best to let people believe that you understood nothing.

'Here we are,' he said suddenly. 'Here's something that might interest you. Some big bets on Leiden. There are three bets of half a million guilders.' That was almost £200,000.

I went round to look at the computer screen. The bets had been placed by a betting syndicate, or group, and there were no names of people. The bets had been placed in Amsterdam, Leiden and Rotterdam. The name of the syndicate was the Amsterdam Connection.

The name meant nothing to me.

'Wow!' I said. 'One and a half million guilders ... that's over half a million pounds in total ... That's a really big bet. Is that usual?'

'Well,' said Ronnie, 'it's not that common, but it does happen. And it's allowed. We never ask questions – it's not our job.'

The Amsterdam Connection were probably very happy that no one asked questions. At six to one, they had made about £3,000,000! Not bad for a night's work.

I asked Ronnie for a list of all the bets placed by the Amsterdam Connection in the past year. He said it would take him a day. I said I'd be back next morning, early.

'Oh, and tonight's match too. I want to find out if there are any large bets on Barcelona,' I said as I left.

I went back to the hotel and lay on my bed to think. I turned on the TV. There was a football match on. I didn't know who the teams were, but I watched for a while. A blonde-haired striker had the ball. He went past three men and shot at goal. The goalkeeper went to his right to save the ball but missed. The blond guy had scored a fantastic goal and jumped up and down.

The goalkeeper ... I wondered. I turned off the TV and smiled to myself.

Chapter 10
A policeman

'And what makes you think,' asked de Vries, 'that this betting syndicate, the Amsterdam Connection, has got anything to do with Mr Christiaans?'

I was talking to Inspector Joop de Vries, head of the Amsterdam Police Murder Squad, at police headquarters on Elandsgracht. It was time, I had decided, to see if we could work together. But he was a tall unsmiling man and he wasn't easy to talk to – I could see why Elly didn't like him.

'It's a guess,' I said, 'but I think it's worth looking into.'

De Vries stared at me. He wasn't a man who liked to guess. I could see that I wasn't getting anywhere. And it wasn't very pleasant sitting in his office. It was filled with cigarette smoke and his desk was a mess.

'And then there's this guy that I met in de Pijp ...' I said.

'This guy?' de Vries asked, putting another cigarette in his mouth.

'Yes. I can't tell you his name, but – '

'Miss Jensen,' said de Vries, trying to be patient,

'how can I accept the word of someone whose name I do not know?'

There was silence for a moment. I wanted to leave right then, but decided to try a little longer.

'But he says that Max Carson was already dead when he arrived in de Pijp,' I said, 'and the guy that you've got, this Schaap guy – he just stole his wallet.'

De Vries said nothing.

'And then I was attacked, on the street outside my hotel,' I said. 'Somebody was trying to frighten me.'

I was sure that whoever had attacked me was trying to stop me from finding the truth.

'I'm very sorry about that Miss Jensen,' said de Vries. 'Amsterdam is quite a safe city, but these things do happen.'

I wondered how I was going to make this man understand.

'And the evidence?' he continued, blowing cigarette smoke over his desk into my face. 'Where's your evidence? The only thing you have is the story of a man who is almost certainly a criminal himself.'

'I don't have any evidence yet. That's my problem,' I said calmly. 'Anyway, I'm not a policewoman, Inspector, I'm a news reporter. You're the ones who are supposed to find the evidence,' I reminded him.

That was a mistake. De Vries was not the kind of guy who liked to be told how to do his job. 'Now look, Miss Jensen,' he said, suddenly sitting up straight. 'I suggest you keep to your job and I'll keep to mine. We work with evidence around here. As you say, you are not a policewoman. Perhaps it's best to keep out of it. You people just make our job more difficult,' he added.

The police were the same in Holland as they were in England, I thought. Always complaining about reporters.

'Look, Inspector,' I said, trying to stay calm, 'I've come here to give you some information. There's nothing in it for me. I just thought you might look into it.'

I stood up to leave. I got the feeling that I was talking to myself and wasting a lot of time. I had to get hold of some evidence. I left de Vries in his smoky office sitting at his messy desk. I had a football match to see.

Chapter 11
A football match

'Who's the Rotterdam goalkeeper?' I asked Jos van Essen as we drove to Rotterdam in his white Porsche.

'Raúl Sanchez,' he said. 'Why?'

'Tell me about him,' I said.

'A great goalkeeper, a nice guy,' said Jos.

'No, I mean … his family and things,' I said.

'Oh, well. He comes from Colombia. His family were very poor. I think when the Carson School found him, he was a boy of eight or nine. He was working on the street in Bogotá,' said Jos, as he turned onto the motorway to Rotterdam.

'And the Carson School arranged for his whole family to come to Holland, right?' I asked.

'No, not exactly. They still live over there, but Raúl has enough money for them to live comfortably now.'

That was a big responsibility for a young man, I thought. Raúl Sanchez had to make sure that his family were all right.

Since watching the match on television I had

been thinking a lot about goalkeepers. Strikers were important when it came to winning and losing matches, but goalkeepers were important too. If you wanted a team to lose a match, the goalkeeper was the man for the job.

Jos and I chatted about this and that as we drove to Rotterdam. Jos told me about his plans for the future. Perhaps he would go to England to manage a football team and start a new life there. He'd had offers from some big clubs.

At about 6:50 we arrived at Rotterdam Football Club. We left the car in the car park and went towards the stadium.

'We must hurry,' said Jos, 'or we'll miss the start of the match.'

We went into the crowded stadium and found our seats. As an ex-player, Jos had tickets for the best seats. I looked around. There were probably fifty thousand people. There was a lot of noise with the fans of both teams singing and shouting.

Less than a minute after we'd sat down, the referee blew his whistle and the match started. Rotterdam played well in the first half of the match and got the first goal. Their star striker, Ritter, scored with his favourite left foot, the ball flying into the corner of the goal. The Barcelona goalkeeper went towards the ball, but couldn't reach it. At half time the score was 1–0 to Rotterdam. The Rotterdam fans screamed and shouted.

In the second half, it was Barcelona who played better, though for a while nobody shot at goal. Then, after about seventy-five minutes' play, their great striker, Martínez, finally started a run. He went round one, two, three men. The Barcelona fans screamed, 'Martínez! Martíez!' Martínez was in front of the goal. He shot into the top right-hand corner. The Rotterdam goalkeeper, Sanchez, jumped towards the ball but it went through his fingers and into the goal. It was 1–1! The Barcelona fans went crazy.

Then, about ten minutes later, Martínez scored again. Again, Sanchez touched the ball, but it went through his fingers. Sanchez wasn't playing well at all. The Barcelona fans went even more crazy! Then the referee blew the final whistle. Barcelona had won 2–1!

We hurried out of the stadium as quickly as we could, trying to avoid the crowds. 'Thank you,' I said to Jos as he started the car to go back to Amsterdam. 'It was great!' Even though Rotterdam had lost, it had been exciting. I hadn't been to a football match since Max had taken me to see Manchester United years before.

Jos didn't look too happy. 'Barcelona are a great team, but Rotterdam should have won. Well, let's hope they do better against Ajax.'

'When are they playing Ajax?' I asked. Ajax were the team from Amsterdam.

'Saturday,' Jos answered. 'Only three days away. And it's a big one. It's important Rotterdam win.'

We drove back to Amsterdam, talking about the match.

Finally we reached the Continental. As the car stopped outside the hotel, Jos said, 'Oh, I've got something for you, Kate.'

He picked up a large brown envelope lying on the back seat. In the envelope was a copy of the photograph I had seen at Jos's apartment in Oude Schans – the photo of the Rotterdam team.

'I saw you liked it,' he said, smiling. 'So here's one for you.' He handed it to me.

'Oh, thank you,' I said. 'That's really kind of you, Jos. Could you sign your name on the back for me, perhaps with a little message?'

'Of course.' Jos pulled a pen out of his pocket and turned the photograph over. 'What would you like me to write?'

'Why not "To my friend, Kate"?' I suggested.

'My dear friend,' said Jos, smiling.

He wrote the message, put the photograph back in the envelope and gave it to me. 'Good night, Kate,' he said.

I got out of the car and watched him drive away. Then I took the photograph out of the envelope and looked down at it. It read: 'To my dear freind Kate, with love from Jos.'

My mind was racing. So Jos was my 'freind'. He knew, or thought he knew, something about what was going on. I just hoped his information was better than his spelling.

I walked into the hotel lost in thought. I needed to speak to Jos. I decided I would go and see him the next day.

But the next day never came for Jos van Essen. That night he was found dead outside his apartment on Oude Schans.

Chapter 12
A goalkeeper

'Let's start with the Amsterdam Connection,' I said to Raúl Sanchez, the goalkeeper at Rotterdam City Football Club.

'What?' he asked.

Sanchez was a handsome man with dark brown skin and lots of curly black hair. His brown eyes looked surprised, but I had a feeling that he knew exactly what I was talking about. I explained, though, just to make really sure.

'The Amsterdam Connection,' I explained, 'is the name of a syndicate, a group of people who are putting big money on football teams that play against Rotterdam City. They're making millions.'

I was talking to Sanchez at his house just outside Amsterdam. It was Friday. Jos van Essen had been found, stabbed to death outside his apartment the day before. His wallet had gone. Again, the killing looked just like a mugging. I was angry and I wanted answers.

'I don't know what you're talking about, Miss

Jensen,' said Sanchez. 'I think you'd better leave.' He got up.

'Sit down,' I said. 'I'm not going anywhere until I find out what's going on.'

The goalkeeper sat down.

'Listen Raúl, and listen well,' I continued seriously. 'Two of my friends are dead and I'm angry. Very angry. I know that someone is betting large amounts of money on Rotterdam losing matches.'

'And so?' he asked.

'I know that you are a great goalkeeper who played like a five-year-old last night. I also know,' I added, just so that he understood clearly, 'that if I tell the police what I know and you don't help them, that you will go to prison for a very long time. And I will tell the police. You'll lose your career as a footballer and your family will be poor again. You choose.'

I looked at him. He sat staring down at his feet. He didn't say anything for a long time, but finally I saw that my words were beginning to work. Or perhaps it was Jos van Essen's death that was helping the Rotterdam goalkeeper to see that he was playing a dangerous game.

'Well, yes ...' said Sanchez, taking a deep breath.

'I've been offered a lot of money to, you know, lose matches.'

Sanchez looked unhappy.

'You were asked to lose matches?' I repeated.

I knew it happened sometimes in football and in other sports. Back in England, there had been a big case with a London club about two years before. Criminals had offered famous players money to lose matches: to miss goals if they were strikers or miss the ball if they were goalkeepers. Then the criminals put a lot of money on the other team to win. They had made millions of pounds that way before they were caught. And of course the players could get sent to prison, too.

'Yes,' said Sanchez quietly, 'but ...'

'But you want to stop, right?' I asked.

The goalkeeper nodded.

'And you were asked to lose matches by Tom Carson?' I asked.

'No, no, not Mr Carson,' he said.

'Well, who was it?' I asked.

'Christiaans,' he said. 'Martijn Christiaans.' I looked across at Sanchez. His face had gone almost white – he was a frightened man.

So that's what Christiaans was doing: taking over the club and making millions for himself, possibly with the help of some friends. But why was Tom Carson letting him do it? Perhaps Tom Carson, too, was frightened of Christiaans. But why?

'Does Tom know what Christiaans is doing?' I asked.

'Yes, of course ... Well, he must know,' said Sanchez. 'But he can't do anything to stop him, I'm not sure why, but he just can't.'

'So why didn't you go to the police at the start?' I said.

'I was too frightened,' said Sanchez.

'Frightened?' I asked.

'Of course,' he said, looking worried. 'I could lose everything. I have four brothers and sisters who would have to leave school and go back on the street. And my mother would be very poor again.'

Poor Sanchez. He was in an impossible situation.

'And Christiaans is a dangerous guy,' he added, his brown eyes growing larger. 'I mean very dangerous. You saw what happened to Max and Jos van Essen.'

It was obvious why everyone was frightened.

'I've known for a long time that I have to stop

this,' said the Rotterdam goalkeeper. 'I just don't know how.'

'And the match against Ajax tomorrow,' I said. 'Have you been asked to lose that one as well?'

'Yes,' he said quietly. Again fear came into his eyes.

'Don't worry,' I said to Sanchez. 'I think we can do something. But we have to act quickly and we need some evidence, something to show the police.'

Once again, my only hope was Elly. I rang her.

'Listen, Elly,' I said, 'I need your help again.'

'Well, I'm busy right now, Kate,' she said. 'I can be there in an hour.'

I gave her the address of Sanchez's house and put the phone down.

An hour later Elly was sitting looking at Sanchez and me, listening carefully. I told her the whole story. I could see from her face that she believed me.

'So, Elly,' I asked, 'do you think you can get us a tape recorder and a microphone? You know, the kind you can put in a pocket or something.'

I knew that the police used tiny microphones and tape recorders that you could hide in bags, or pockets, or even attach to a person's clothes. Elly said she thought she could get one.

'Elly,' I said, 'there's another thing.'

'Yes?' she asked.

'Max Carson had a bad heart. Jos told me that he took pills. I need to know if the police found the pills in his room or on his body. I need to know how many pills were in the bottle, the name of the chemist where he got them and the date,' I said.

'Is that all?' she asked.

'Yeah, and if you could get the information quickly ...' I said, giving her my sweetest smile.

Chapter 13
A plan

Elly returned an hour later with the tape recorder and microphone.

'Now here's what I want you to do,' I said to Raúl. 'We're going to attach this microphone and tape recorder to the inside of your jacket. Just remember to stay close to Christiaans while he's speaking.'

Then Raúl rang Christiaans and arranged to see him at his house. 'I just want to talk about something,' said Raúl cheerfully.

When he got to Christiaans' house, Raúl was going to tell him that he wanted more money for playing badly. We all hoped that Christiaans would talk, say something about what he was doing while Raúl taped him. It was very dangerous for Raúl, but if it worked it would give us the evidence we needed.

'I'll go with Raúl,' said Elly. 'I'll wait nearby.'

After the interview with Christiaans, Elly could also make sure that Raúl didn't get hurt. She had brought some jeans and a blouse and she now changed from her policewoman's uniform.

'Oh,' I added, 'and what about the pills? Did you find out anything?'

'Yes, the police did find some pills in Max's room,' she said. 'They were called Lanoxin. They were bought from a chemist in The Hague two weeks ago. The full bottle was sixty pills and you have to take just one a day. There were about thirty left when they found them.'

Lanoxin ... Lanoxin ... I knew that name from somewhere, but right now I couldn't remember where.

Elly and Raúl left. It was time for me to go and see Ronnie at Kanters.

I took a taxi to the Kanters office. When I got there, Ronnie was sitting at his computer, exactly as I had seen him yesterday. It was like he never went home. He had a computer print-out of the information I needed.

I looked at the print-out. It was very interesting reading. There were, as I had thought, regular bets against Rotterdam over the past year made by the Amsterdam Connection. There was also a large bet on Barcelona to win Wednesday's match. The Amsterdam Connection had done it again. However, a far larger amount of money was on the Rotterdam-Ajax match taking place the next day.

I put the computer print-out in an envelope and posted it to my hotel, with my name on it. That way, whatever happened, it would arrive at the hotel tomorrow.

I went back to the hotel to wait for Elly and Raúl to come back. I ordered some tea from room service and waited. I drank my tea. An hour went by. Then two hours. As time went on I became more and more worried. Where were they? We had arranged to meet back at the hotel as soon as they had the tape with the evidence on it. I tried to read, then watch TV, but I couldn't. My mind filled up with terrible ideas of what had happened to them.

I lay on my bed and tried to relax. The name of Max's pills came into my head again. Lanoxin. Yes! That was it! Lanoxin contains digoxin, a powerful heart drug which can kill you if you take too much of it. I had first heard about Lanoxin during a story in London. A doctor had killed his wife using it. It's perfect for killing someone because digoxin can't be found in the body after about twelve hours. Perhaps someone had made Max take a lot of Lanoxin pills and killed him that way! Perhaps Bert was right after all. Perhaps Max had been dead before someone knifed him in de Pijp.

Then, finally, at about seven o'clock, there was a knock at the door. Thank God, I thought. I jumped up and opened it, expecting to see Elly and Raúl. Suddenly I was pushed back into the room. A tall man in a black suit moved quickly through the door and put his hand over my mouth. It was the same man who had attacked me outside the hotel three days ago. The same dark hair and clear blue eyes.

'Christiaans?' I asked.

'Keep quiet!' he said into my ear. 'Or I'll kill you.'

I took that as a 'yes'.

Chapter 14 Prisoner

Christiaans pushed me to the other side of the room. I saw that he was holding a gun. 'Where is it?' he said.

'Where's what?' I asked, trying to look calm.

'The print-out!' he said. 'I've just visited your friend Ronnie and I don't think he'll be helping you any more. Now where is it?'

'Where are Elly and Raúl? What have you done to them?' I shouted. I was angry.

He smiled an ugly smile. 'They're fine,' he said. 'But they are very stupid. Raúl should know better than to go against me, and your policewoman friend should stay away from things she knows nothing about.'

'Where are they?' I said again. I wanted to hit him but the gun was pointing right at me.

'They're quite safe. We need Raúl to be fit if he's going to play his best, or should I say worst, for us tomorrow.'

'He'll never do it,' I said.

'Oh, I think he will,' said Christiaans, smiling

again. 'If he wants you and Elly to live.'

'It'll never work,' I said. 'Elly will be missed at police headquarters.'

'It's Saturday tomorrow,' he said. 'Who'll miss her? By the time anyone misses her or you, the match will be over, I'll be a multimillionaire and I'll be far away from here. Now,' he continued, looking serious again, 'it's time you joined your friends. I need you safely out of the way until the match is over. Come on, we're going for a little walk outside. And remember, this gun is pointing at you. If you make any noise at all, it will be a pleasure to shoot you.'

Before we left the room, he hid the gun under his coat and held it against my back. Then he pushed me out of the door, down the stairs and through the back door of the hotel. He was tall and strong. With him standing just behind me and his gun in my back, it would be stupid to try anything. Outside the hotel he pushed me into the back of a small van with dark windows. Then there was nothing.

* * *

The first thing I noticed was the pain; a terrible pain starting at the back of my head and finishing over my eyes.

At first it seemed as if I was in complete darkness. Then my eyes got used to it and above me I could see a little light coming from a window. It was hard to think with the pain in my head, but I guessed that I was lying on the floor of a room under a house, a cellar perhaps. The floor was made of stone and it was hard, dirty and cold.

I checked my body. This was difficult because I was handcuffed – my hands held together in front of me. The hard metal of the handcuffs cut into my hands. Other than the terrible headache, I seemed to be OK. Then my eyes got more used to the dark and I looked around the room. There, in the corner, was Elly, wearing handcuffs and with something over her mouth so that she couldn't speak. Her eyes were shut, but I saw that she was breathing; she wasn't dead but I guessed she was unconscious. She had blood running from her head. I wondered where Raúl was.

I had to think and act quickly. What would happen once the match was over and Christiaans had his money? I couldn't see someone like Christiaans letting us go. I was quite sure he'd kill us anyway. Maybe he'd make our murders look like senseless stabbings, leaving our bodies in the street at night.

That was what he had done with Max and Jos. From what he had said, he obviously had a flight booked to some country far away once the match was over. Perhaps he'd just leave us in this cellar to die.

I went to Elly and spoke to her. At first she didn't move but then, slowly, her eyes opened a little. She looked at me as if she hardly knew me.

'Listen, Elly,' I whispered. 'It's me, Kate. I'm going to try to get out of here, but I'll come back soon, OK? I'll come back with help.'

Her eyes closed again.

I heard voices somewhere. I knew that I didn't have much time. I had to get out of here, and find a way of getting Elly out, too. It seemed impossible.

I looked up again towards the window. Yes, I thought, we were in a cellar and that window probably faced the street. There would also probably be steps which led up to the street. These cellars were very common in Amsterdam. The window was about two metres above me and very small. Luckily it was open a little and there was a stone shelf just beneath it. It wasn't very wide, but it was just wide enough perhaps. If only I could reach that shelf! But how? And even if I could manage to reach it, how was I going to get through the window? I was quite slim, but the window looked very small.

I walked slowly to the wall where the window was and felt it with the back of my hand. I moved my hands slowly up the wall, trying to find somewhere I could place a foot. There was nothing.

I moved backwards, away from the window, towards a corner of the room. As I moved in the darkness I almost fell over something behind me. It was a chair! It was old and it didn't seem very strong, but it was a chair. I started to pull it carefully towards the little window. It was my only hope.

It was hard to move the chair without making any noise. Any movement on the floor made a lot of noise and the metal handcuffs stopped me from lifting the chair. I tried to breathe slowly. It took a long time but finally the chair was in position under the window. It was time to try it out, to see if it would take my weight. If it wasn't strong enough and I fell, the people upstairs would certainly hear the noise and come running to the cellar. It would be the end.

First I sat on it. It was fine. Then I stepped up onto the chair, slowly and carefully. To my surprise it didn't break. I reached up to the window and managed to touch it. It was dark outside, and I guessed it must be very late. I must have been unconscious for a long time.

Just then I heard a low noise behind me. I turned. It was Elly trying to speak.

'Shh! Elly,' I whispered. 'I'll be back soon, I promise.' As I said it, I wondered whether it was true, whether I could really promise that.

I turned back towards the window. I felt the night air coming through it and heard the sound of traffic somewhere. Rain, too. It had started raining. Perhaps I could get through the window, I thought. I would have to pull myself up as hard as I could. If I fell back onto the chair there would be a lot of noise and we would be finished.

I reached up and pulled as hard as I could. I slowly managed to lift myself up onto the shelf just below the window. My arms were strong after all the years of karate training. I felt the fresh air on my face. I breathed it in, trying to give myself new strength. I looked back at Elly. If I could escape, perhaps I could get help.

I pushed through the window, handcuffed hands first, then head. I could see the ground just a metre below me. But would I get through that tiny window?

I pushed my knees against the shelf, breathing heavily. I gave one final strong push and I was out! I pushed my hands down to the ground and fell on my shoulder. I had been right about the steps. I was lying at the bottom of about ten stone steps. I stood up quickly and ran up the steps and out onto the street. I looked up at the house. I had seen it before – it was Christiaans' house on Herengracht. I ran as fast as I could down the street. It was raining very hard now. I just kept on running.

I ran all the way to the central police station on Elandsgracht. The young policeman at the desk looked at me very strangely as I ran through the door. I was wet from head to foot and wearing handcuffs. I quickly told the policeman what was happening as he took the handcuffs off. 'We have to get back to Herengracht quickly,' I said. 'Very quickly! Christiaans is dangerous!'

The policeman called three other policemen. I got into a car with two of them and two others followed in another car. As we drove to Herengracht, I told the policemen more of the story. I told them I didn't know where Raúl was and that I was worried about him. Five minutes later, we parked just round the corner from Christiaans' house.

Two of the policemen went round to the front of the house; the other two ran off round the back. The idea was that as the two policemen rang the bell at the front of the house, the two at the back would kick the door down and rescue Elly.

I sat in the car, shaking with the cold. The policeman had given me a blanket and I pulled it around me, trying to get warm. I could see the two policemen at the back of the house. There was a loud noise as they broke the door down. Then there was silence. Each minute seemed like an hour. Suddenly I heard a gunshot! Who had been shot? 'Please, God, don't let it be Elly,' I said to myself. I listened for more shots, but I heard nothing.

Finally, after about fifteen minutes, two of the policemen came out of the house with Christiaans handcuffed. There was blood coming from Christiaans' leg. I sat forward, hoping that I would soon see Elly. Then, a few moments later, the other two policemen came out with Elly. Behind her was Raúl! So he had been in the house all the time! He looked OK. Elly looked pretty bad, but she was alive.

One of the policemen helped Elly into the car next to me and Raúl got in on the other side.

'Thank God you're safe,' I said and took hold of Elly's hand.

She gave me a weak smile.

'So what happened?' I asked them.

'Well, everything went as planned,' said Raúl. 'Christiaans talked to me and I left his house with the tape.'

'Yes,' said Elly, 'and then Raúl came outside and round the corner to meet me. But Christiaans followed him. He had a gun and made us go back to his house. I think Christiaans was very clever. He probably realised that something was going on as soon as Raúl said he wanted to visit him.'

'When we got back into the house, he knocked Elly out and locked me in another room,' said Raúl. 'He needed me to play in the match. And he needed Elly – he told me that he'd kill her if I didn't play and lose the match against Ajax.'

It was lucky that Raúl was an important part of Christiaans' plan. If he hadn't been, both he and Elly would probably have been killed there and then.

Chapter 15
Stories

It was 3:00 in the morning and I was sitting in de Vries's smoky office with Elly. She had seen a doctor at the police station and was feeling a little better. De Vries was angry that she had put herself in so much danger, but mainly he was just happy that she was OK.

Raúl had told his whole story to de Vries and was allowed to go home. He would have to give evidence later, but he probably wouldn't be sent to prison.

My head was hurting, but at last I was giving de Vries the evidence he wanted, the evidence that would send Christiaans to prison for a very long time.

'Max Carson wouldn't play Christiaans' game,' I said. 'Max had found out what was going on. He tried to get Christiaans to stop, but he couldn't. My guess is that Christiaans was the person Max was going to visit that Thursday evening. Probably to tell him to stop or to warn him that he would tell the police. Christiaans couldn't allow that so he killed him.'

'So he stabbed Max in his house?' de Vries asked.

'No,' I answered. 'The guy I met in de Pijp was right; Max was dead before he was knifed. Somehow

Christiaans made Max take far too much Lanoxin, Max's heart pills. Perhaps he put the pills into a drink.'

I told him about digoxin; about how you couldn't find it in the body after twelve hours. 'There were a lot of pills missing from Max's bottle,' I said.

'But why then stab him?' de Vries asked.

'Well, Christiaans had a body to get rid of somehow,' I explained. 'He didn't want to leave it in the street just like it was because the police would wonder how Max had died. You would probably have done a postmortem immediately and found the drug still in Max's body. Christiaans decided it would be much safer to make you think Max had been stabbed to death by a street criminal.'

'And it almost worked,' said Elly. 'By the time the postmortem was done, the drug couldn't be found.'

De Vries looked at me. 'And van Essen?' he asked.

'Well, unfortunately he knew too much,' I said. 'He'd refused to take money from Christiaans and had tried to keep out of it. He even left the football club that he loved. I think he was very sad to see what was happening to football. He had his dreams ...

'But it was hard to just forget about it,' I

continued. 'He liked Max and he knew that he was in a difficult situation. And then Max was killed and Jos was sure Christiaans had murdered him ... And then I came.' I stopped. I wondered whether Jos van Essen would still be alive if I hadn't arrived in Amsterdam, if I hadn't made him part of it again. I suddenly felt very sad.

'And,' I added, 'you can see the evidence about the Amsterdam Connection when it arrives in the post tomorrow – I mean today!'

Christiaans had probably destroyed the evidence on the computer at Kanters, but at least there was a paper copy. Then I remembered Ronnie. What had happened to him?

'He's OK,' said de Vries. 'Christiaans hurt him a little and frightened him a lot, but he didn't kill him.'

'And what about the rest of the Amsterdam Connection?' I asked. I guessed that Christiaans had about three or four 'friends' who were part of the syndicate.

De Vries smiled. 'We're looking for them now, Miss Jensen,' he said.

'There's just one thing that I don't really understand,' Elly said. 'Why did Tom Carson allow

Christiaans to buy up his club?'

'Yes,' I said. 'I'd like to know that, too.'

'Well, why don't we ask him?' said de Vries. 'He's in the interview room next door. I'll bring him in.' De Vries got up and left the room.

Elly and I looked at each other. My head was hurting, but I wanted to talk to him. I had to talk to him. Soon de Vries returned with Tom Carson behind him. Tom looked pleased to see me. He was a much happier man than when I had last seen him.

'Miss Jensen,' he said, 'I'm so happy it's all over.' He smiled a big smile and sat down across the table from us.

'But why did you let Christiaans take over the club?' I asked. 'I don't understand.'

'I didn't have any choice,' said Carson. 'The club wasn't doing very well. We were very good in the late eighties, early nineties, then we started to go down. We lost some of our best players. We needed some money to buy new players, really good players. And to rebuild the stadium.'

I remembered that the stadium I had seen was new – and beautiful.

'We looked everywhere, but no-one wanted to put

money into the club. Then Christiaans came along,' Carson continued. 'He offered to put a lot of money into the club. But of course he wanted shares, ten per cent at first.'

Carson took a deep breath. 'The club is my whole life,' he said. 'I started it twenty years ago, a few years after I stopped playing. It was my dream, you know, to have a club and a school ... to really put something back into Dutch football. I couldn't let Rotterdam City Football Club just die. I love it too much.'

Tom Carson took another deep breath.

'So,' he continued, 'everything was fine at first. But soon Christiaans started asking for more,' he said. 'And then things started happening ... but for a long time I didn't know exactly what Christiaans was doing.'

'When did you find out about the Amsterdam Connection?' I asked.

'About a year ago,' he said. 'But by then Christiaans had forty-five per cent of the club and he was in a strong position. He said if I went to the police he would tell them I had been part of the syndicate too. Christiaans said the police would never believe I knew nothing about it. And I thought Max would think of something ... He always thought of something.'

Tom Carson smiled sadly. Christiaans had been too strong, even for Max.

'And well ... you know the rest,' said Tom. 'Max thought we should tell the police, but I wasn't sure. We argued about it. I didn't want to go to the police because I knew how dangerous Christiaans was. I was frightened for myself and the players.'

'And what are you going to do now?' I asked.

'Get back to the club and try to really make it work.' He smiled.

I shook Tom's hand. 'Good luck, Tom,' I said. 'I'm sure you'll do it.'

I was tired. I got up to leave.

'Miss Jensen,' said de Vries, smiling at last and holding out his hand. 'Thank you.'

I smiled back. The inspector was not an easy man, but he knew that he'd been wrong. I smiled at de Vries, but I didn't feel very happy. I had wanted to give him the evidence, to show him that I had been right, but now that I was here it didn't seem so important. I could only think about Max and Jos; they were dead and nothing would bring them back.

Chapter 16
Goodbye Amsterdam

I opened the door of de Vries's office. I had been awake all night and I was beginning to feel it. Elly followed me out.

'Are you going back to the hotel?' she asked.

'Yes,' I said. 'I've got a story to write if I still want my job in London.' I smiled at her and added, 'Oh, and Elly, thanks for everything. You've been a real friend.'

She put her arms around me. 'Yeah, thank you too, Kate,' said Elly. 'And Kate ...'

'Mmm?'

'Don't come back to Amsterdam for a while, eh? I don't think I can take it.' She laughed.

I kissed Elly and left the police station. I walked back to the hotel through the city's empty streets. They were safe for me now that Christiaans was in a police cell. The salt smell of the sea cleared my head and the morning light danced on the water of the canals. Amsterdam was beautiful once more.

As I walked back I thought about the people I was leaving behind in Amsterdam: Elly, who had put herself in so much danger to help me; Raúl who had finally been brave enough to do what was right; my poor 'freind' Jos who had lost his life and Tom Carson who had lost his brother. I looked into the dark water of the canal and thought about Max. Max had saved my life all those years ago. He had fought for me when I needed it. And I had to fight for him when he couldn't fight for himself. Perhaps that was the meaning of friendship. Perhaps the only true one.

I wrote my story. An hour later, at 8:30 in the morning, it was finished. I faxed it through to the office back in London. It would be waiting for Balzano when he got into work.

I lay on my bed. I was exhausted and fell asleep. The phone woke me up. It was Balzano, shouting, but this time he was happy. 'Great story, Jensen!'

'Thanks,' I said. 'Oh, and Dave, I'd like to take two weeks off. I need a holiday.'

I held the telephone away from my ear and smiled. Some things never changed.

After reading

读后活动

Choose some of these activities.

1. Which characters did you like most? Why?

2. Imagine you are making a film of the book. Which actors would you choose to play the main characters? Would you make any changes to the story?

3. Imagine Kate Jensen interviews Raúl after the match against Barcelona. Write the interview.

4. Write the conversation between Raúl and Christiaans in Chapter 13, when Raúl has the microphone and tape recorder.

5. Write a letter to the author, Sue Leather, telling her what you liked or didn't like about the book.

6. What happens after the end of the story? Write an extra chapter.

7. Write Kate Jensen's story for the *Daily Echo* about the Amsterdam Connection.

8. Make your own activities for other students to do, e.g. write some True/False questions.

Learning guide | 学习指导

Chapter 1

New words 生词

- boxer /ˈbɒksə(r)/ *n.* 拳击运动员，拳击手
- boxing /ˈbɒksɪŋ/ *n.* 拳击
- chase /tʃeɪs/ *v.* 追赶；追捕
- crime /kraɪm/ *n.* 罪行，犯罪
- Dutch /dʌtʃ/ *n.* 荷兰人；荷兰语 *a.* 荷兰的；荷兰人的；荷兰语的
- explode /ɪkˈspləʊd/ *v.* 爆炸；爆发
- karate /kəˈrɑːti/ *n.* 空手道
- share /ʃeə(r)/ *n.* 股份
- temper /ˈtempə(r)/ *n.* 脾气，性情
- tough /tʌf/ *a.* 艰苦的，艰难的

Phrases & expressions 短语和表达

- crazy about ... 热衷于……，对……感到狂热
- make a name 成名，出名

Cultural notes 文化点滴

- Amsterdam: 阿姆斯特丹，荷兰首都及最大城市，位于荷兰西北部。阿姆斯特丹有许多著名旅游景点，包括历史悠久的运河网、荷兰国家博物馆、梵高博物馆等。

- Manchester United: 曼彻斯特联队足球俱乐部，位于英国曼彻斯特市，英文全称为 Manchester United Football Club，简称 ManUtd 或 MUFC，中文简称“曼联”。曼联是英格兰足球史上最成功的俱乐部之一，也是欧洲乃至世界上最具影响力、最成功的足球队之一。
- Rotterdam: 鹿特丹，荷兰第二大城市，同时也是欧洲最大的海港，位于南荷兰省。

Reading exercise 阅读练习

Look at the words in italics. Who or what is *he, it, you, me, he*?

a) In fact, *he* was famous for his bad temper.

b) I got the feeling that he didn't really want to talk about *it*.

c) 'Listen, why don't *you* come and write a story about our club in Holland?'

d) 'You know *me*, Max, I only write about crime.'

e) Two days later, *he* was found lying dead in an Amsterdam street ...

Chapter 2

New words 生词

- addict /ˈædɪkt/ *n.* （吸毒）成瘾者；有瘾的人
- arrangement /əˈreɪndʒmənt/ *n.* 商定，约定
- break-in /ˈbreɪkɪn/ *n.* 闯入，非法进入
- colleague /ˈkɒliːg/ *n.* 同事
- contract /ˈkɒntrækt/ *n.* 协议，合同
- criminal /ˈkrɪmɪnl/ *n.* 罪犯
- gang /gæŋ/ *n.* 一帮，一伙（罪犯）

- mugger /ˈmʌɡə(r)/ *n.* 行凶抢劫者
- mugging /ˈmʌɡɪŋ/ *n.* 抢劫
- sweaty /ˈsweti/ *a.* 出汗的，多汗的
- violent /ˈvaɪələnt/ *a.* 暴力的
- witness /ˈwɪtnəs/ *n.* 目击者，见证人 *v.* 目睹，目击

Phrases & expressions 短语和表达

- come to an arrangement with somebody 与某人达成协议
- look somebody straight in the eyes 直视某人
- make no sense 讲不通，毫无意义
- red-light district 红灯区

Reading exercises 阅读练习

1. Match the beginnings and endings.
   1) Kate couldn't understand why
   2) Kate wrote a story about a gang murder
   3) As a result of this story
   4) Max put his life in danger
   5) Dave Balzano finally agreed

   ______a) in order to save Kate.
   ______b) she was kept prisoner by the gang.
   ______c) to let Kate go to Amsterdam.
   ______d) when she worked in Manchester.
   ______e) Max had been murdered.
2. Why do you think Max was murdered?

Chapter 3

New words 生词

- apparently /əˈpærəntli/ *ad.* 明显地
- attacker /əˈtækə(r)/ *n.* 攻击者
- canal /kəˈnæl/ *n.* 运河
- cyclist /ˈsaɪklɪst/ *n.* 骑自行车的人
- inn /ɪn/ *n.* 客栈，小旅馆
- postmortem /ˌpəʊstˈmɔːtəm/ *n.* 尸检
- squad /skwɒd/ *n.* 小组，小队
- stabbing /ˈstæbɪŋ/ *n.* 持刀刺伤
- tulip /ˈtjuːlɪp/ *n.* 郁金香

Phrases & expressions 短语和表达

- check in 登记入住
- fight back 反抗
- in charge of ... 负责……

Cultural notes 文化点滴

- Keizersgratcht: 皇帝运河，阿姆斯特丹市中心主要运河之一，也是其中最宽的一条。阿姆斯特丹的运河总长度超过 100 千米，拥有大约 90 座岛屿和 1500 座桥梁，使得该市被称为“北方的威尼斯”。阿姆斯特丹的运河体系由四条相互平行的弧形运河组成，呈半月形环绕着市中心，它们由外向内分别是辛格尔运河（Singelgracht）、王子运河（Prinsengratcht）、皇帝运河和绅士运河（Herengracht）。

• koffe verkeerd: 滴漏咖啡或浓缩咖啡（需要加两倍的热牛奶）。verkeerd 在荷兰语中的意思是"错误的"，因为大部分荷兰人认为喝咖啡应该少放或不放牛奶。

• Schiphol Airport: 阿姆斯特丹史基浦机场，荷兰乃至欧洲的主要机场之一，也是进出荷兰的主要门户。该机场于 1967 年 4 月建成并投入运营。

• The Hague: 海牙，位于南荷兰省，同时也是该省省会。海牙是仅次于阿姆斯特丹和鹿特丹的荷兰第三大城市。虽然海牙并不是荷兰的首都，但它是荷兰中央政府所在地，几乎所有的政府机关与外国使馆都位于此。

Reading exercises 阅读练习

1. Match the questions and answers.

   1) 'So, it just looks like it was a mugging that went wrong?'
   2) 'So who found him?'
   3) 'Did the killer take his money, then?'
   4) 'Why didn't he just go back to The Hague?'
   5) 'Who's in charge of Max's case?'

   ______a) ' ... one of the police teams going round the city late Thursday night.'

   ______b) 'Joop de Vries, Murder Squad.'

   ______c) 'He must have had a business meeting the next morning.'

   ______d) 'Well, the police couldn't find his wallet.'

   ______e) 'I'm afraid that's what it looks like, Kate.'

2. Jos van Essen's address was in Max's pocket. Why?

Chapter 4

New words 生词

- block /blɒk/ *n.* 街区
- coach /kəʊtʃ/ *n.* 教练
- intercom /ˈɪntəkɒm/ *n.* 对讲机
- scout /skaʊt/ *n.* 人才发掘者，星探
- striker /ˈstraɪkə(r)/ *n.*（足球）前锋
- trainer /ˈtreɪnə(r)/ *n.* 运动鞋

Cultural notes 文化点滴

- Cruyff: 克鲁伊夫，荷兰优秀的足球运动员和教练。球员时期的克鲁伊夫有着“飞人”的称号，曾三次获得“欧洲足球先生”称号。他的足球教练生涯在执教巴萨期间达到顶峰，被称为“巴萨教父”。
- Dam Square: 达姆广场，也称“大坝广场”，被称为阿姆斯特丹的心脏，是阿姆斯特丹的发祥地。附近有不少景点（如王宫、杜莎夫人蜡像馆和国家纪念碑），也一直是公众集会的地方，是阿姆斯特丹最知名的广场。
- European Cup: 欧洲杯，即欧洲足球锦标赛（European Football Championship），简称欧锦赛、欧洲杯，是一项由欧洲足球协会联盟旗下会员协会参加的最高级别国家级足球赛事。每四年举行一届。
- Pelé: 贝利，20 世纪最伟大的体育明星之一，被称为“球王”。贝利出生在巴西的一个贫寒家庭，一生中获得过无数荣誉，创造过无数纪录。1987 年 6 月被授予国际足联金质勋章；1999 年被国际奥

委会选举为“世纪运动员”，并被《时代》周刊列入“影响 20 世纪的 100 人”之列；2000 年被国际足联评为 20 世纪最佳球员；2012 年获得金足奖颁发的“史上最佳球员”奖。

- Rembrandt: 伦勃朗（1606—1669），欧洲 17 世纪最伟大的画家之一，也是荷兰历史上最伟大的画家，擅长肖像画、风景画、风俗画、宗教画、历史画等。
- Shearer: 阿兰·希勒，英国人。他从小就是足球天才，5 岁时被幼儿园老师预言为“未来的球星”。他是英超联赛总射手榜的第一名，是英格兰史上最优秀的前锋。
- World Cup: 世界杯（FIFA World Cup），即国际足联世界杯，是世界上有着最高荣誉、最高规格、最高竞技水平、最高知名度的足球赛事。每四年举办一次。

Reading exercise 阅读练习

Complete the summary.

Jos van Essen couldn't ________ Max was dead. Max had helped him become a ________ footballer. Jos said that Max and his ________ Tom were close, but they had been ________ recently. Jos and Max had a drink on ________ evening, and Jos gave him his new ________. Max then took a ________ to visit someone. Kate didn't know Max took ________ for his bad ________. Jos didn't want to talk about the ________ at the football club.

Chapter 5

New words 生词

- apron /ˈeɪprən/ *n.* 围裙
- barman /ˈbɑːmən/ *n.* 酒吧服务员
- cassette /kəˈset/ *n.* 盒式磁带
- confess /kənˈfes/ *v.* 承认，坦白
- gazette /gəˈzet/ *n.* 公报；报纸
- gin /dʒɪn/ *n.* 杜松子酒
- jenever /ˈjənevə/ *n.* 荷兰杜松子酒
- saxophone /ˈsæksəfəʊn/ *n.* 萨克斯管
- tram /træm/ *n.* 有轨电车
- walkman /ˈwɔːkmən/ *n.* 随身听

Cultural notes 文化点滴

- Bordeaux: 波尔多葡萄酒。该酒因其柔顺细致的口感享誉世界，有“法国葡萄酒皇后”的美称。这种葡萄酒得名于其产地波尔多——法国第四大城市，该地被称为世界葡萄酒中心。
- John Coltrane: 约翰·柯川，出生于美国的北卡罗来纳州，是爵士乐历史上最伟大的萨克斯管演奏家之一，同时也是一位优秀的音乐革新家。他在 20 世纪六七十年代的爵士乐坛有着巨大的影响。

Reading exercise 阅读练习

Put the events in the right order.

_____ a) Kate told Elly that Jos was frightened.

______ b) Balzano was annoyed about the *Gazette* getting the story first.

______ c) Kate visited the area where Max had been killed.

______ d) Kate was given three days to find a story.

______ e) Elly said the police had probably found the killer.

______ f) In a bar, Kate met an old man called Bert.

______ g) Kate thought Max's murder was not a simple mugging.

Chapter 6

New words 生词

- guilder /ˈɡɪldə(r)/ *n.* 荷兰盾（荷兰原货币单位）
- whisper /ˈwɪspə(r)/ *v.* 耳语，低声说出

Cultural notes 文化点滴

- guilder: 荷兰盾，荷兰以前的货币单位。现在由于荷兰加入欧元区，荷兰盾已经正式退出历史舞台，但在部分地区仍有使用。
- Het Parool: 荷兰《誓言报》，阿姆斯特丹的地方新闻报纸，成立于1940年，首次出版于1941年，主要以报道当地都市新闻为主，另外也报道国内、国际的重要新闻。

Reading exercise 阅读练习

Look at the words in italics. Who is *I, he, they,* etc.?

a) '*I* have some information for you,' he said.

b) ' ... your friend was already dead when *he* was taken to that street.'

c) '*They* say they found my friend's wallet in his apartment.'

d) '*He* just stole the wallet from the dead body.'

e) *I* had no idea whether the information he'd given me was true.

Chapter 7

New words 生词

- croissant /ˈkrwæsɒ̃/ *n.* 羊角面包
- professional /prəˈfeʃənl/ *a.* 职业的
- publicity /pʌbˈlɪsəti/ *n.* 宣传
- slim /slɪm/ *a.* 苗条的，修长的

Phrases & expressions 短语和表达

- care for sb. 照顾某人
- dressing room 更衣室
- get involved 卷入
- warm-up exercises 热身练习
- win against ... 打败……，赢……

Cultural notes 文化点滴

• Ajax: 阿贾克斯，即阿贾克斯·阿姆斯特丹足球俱乐部，创立于1900年，是荷兰历史上最伟大的足球俱乐部，培养了为数众多的球星，包括约翰·克鲁伊夫（Johan Cruyff）、马尔科·范巴斯滕（Marco van Basten）等。

• Barcelona: 巴塞罗那足球俱乐部，中文简称“巴萨”，是现今欧洲乃至世界足坛最成功的俱乐部之一。

• croissant: 羊角面包，法国人的一种传统早点。传说该面包起源

于奥地利维也纳的一家糕点店。据说 1683 年，当时的奥斯曼帝国军队决定在夜间偷袭维也纳，被当地面包房早早起来的面包师傅们发觉。他们拉响了全城警报，从而使敌方的偷袭以失败而告终。为了纪念这次胜利，面包师傅们把面包做成了号角的形状，这种形状也很近似于奥斯曼帝国新月旗帜的标志。1770 年，奥地利公主玛丽 · 安托瓦内特把羊角面包正式带入法国。

Reading exercises 阅读练习

1. Match the beginnings and endings.
   1) Kate travelled to Rotterdam City Football Club
   2) Elly had warned Kate not to get too involved
   3) Tom didn't seem to be confident
   4) Kate was worried that Tom might discover
   5) Tom showed Kate around the football school
   6) Kate thought there was another reason
   ______a) why Tom seemed to be sad.
   ______b) and explained the work that Max had done.
   ______c) but Kate had to find out who had killed Max.
   ______d) to speak to Max's brother Tom.
   ______e) how little she knew about football.
   ______f) about Rotterdam winning against Barcelona.
2. Do you think Rotterdam City will win against Barcelona?

Chapter 8

New words 生词

- detective /dɪˈtektɪv/ *n.* 侦探 *a.* 侦探的
- elbow /ˈelbəʊ/ *n.* 肘部
- pavement /ˈpeɪvmənt/ *n.* 人行道
- screech /skriːtʃ/ *v.* 发出尖锐刺耳的声音

Phrases & expressions 短语和表达

- bet on ... 就……打赌，下赌注于……
- build up 增进，加强
- buy up 收购，全部买进
- fall over 跌倒，摔倒
- in no time 立即，很快
- let go 放开，放手
- make fun of ... 取笑……，嘲弄……
- no doubt 无疑
- on one's knees 双膝跪在地上
- race off 飞奔而去
- take one's breath away 使某人大惊失色

Reading exercises 阅读练习

1. Complete the summary.

Kate discovered that Martijn Christiaans owned ________ per cent of Rotterdam City Football Club. Kate went to visit him, but he wasn't at home. At the hotel, there was a letter for Kate, advising her to look into a bet that ________ would lose to ________. Kate called

________ who agreed to take her to the match against ________. That night someone ________ Kate, but she used her ________ training to fight back.

2. Who do you think attacked Kate?

Chapter 9

New words 生词

- syndicate /ˈsɪndɪkət/ *n.* 企业联合，财团
- whisky /ˈwɪski/ *n.* 威士忌酒

Reading exercises 阅读练习

1. Complete the sentences with numbers and times.

   a) It was ________ per cent certain that Max had died in de Pijp.

   b) Max died between ________ and ________ in the morning.

   c) The Amsterdam Connection had put over £ ________ on Leiden to win.

   d) At ________ to ________, the syndicate had won about £ ________.

   3,000,000　　12:00　　95　　6　　500,000　　1　　3:30

2. Why did Kate wonder about the goalkeeper?

Chapter 10

New words 生词

- headquarters /ˌhedˈkwɔːtəz/ *n.* 总部
- mess /mes/ *n.* 混乱，一团糟

- messy /ˈmesi/ *a.* 凌乱的，邋遢的

Phrases & expressions 短语和表达

- get hold of ... 抓住……
- keep out of ... 置身于……之外；不卷入……

Reading exercise 阅读练习

Write F (fact) or P (possibility)?

a) Christiaans is part of the Amsterdam Connection.______

b) Max was already dead when he was left in de Pijp.______

c) Kate was attacked in the street.______

d) Kate doesn't have any real evidence.______

e) Kate thought the meeting with de Vries was a waste of time.______

f) Schaap didn't kill Max.______

Chapter 11

New words 生词

- motorway /ˈməʊtəweɪ/ *n.* 高速公路
- offer /ˈɒfə(r)/ *n.* 工作机会
- referee /ˌrefəˈriː/ *n.* 裁判
- whistle /ˈwɪsl/ *n.* 口哨

Cultural notes 文化点滴

- Bogotá: 波哥大，哥伦比亚首都，也是哥伦比亚最大的城市。
- Porsche: 保时捷，德国汽车公司和品牌，1931 年由费迪南德・保

时捷创立于斯图加特，以生产高级跑车闻名于世。

Reading exercise 阅读练习

Put the events in the right order.

______ a) Rotterdam played well and scored the first goal.
______ b) In the second half, Barcelona scored two goals.
______ c) Kate noticed a spelling mistake on Jos's photo.
______ d) Kate knew the letter about the bet was from Jos.
______ e) Jos was disappointed about the result of the match.
______ f) Jos talked about the goalkeeper, Raúl Sanchez.

Chapter 12

New words 生词

- attach /əˈtætʃ/ *v.* 把……固定
- career /kəˈrɪə(r)/ *n.* 职业
- chemist /ˈkemɪst/ *n.* 化学家；药剂师
- curly /ˈkɜːli/ *a.*（头发）卷曲的
- microphone /ˈmaɪkrəfəʊn/ *n.* 麦克风

Phrases & expressions 短语和表达

- in an impossible situation 处于无可奈何的境地
- take over 接管

Reading exercise 阅读练习

Write the names in the spaces.

a) ________ had offered ________ money to lose matches.

b) ________ knew what was happening but couldn't do anything about it.

c) ________ knew if he went to the police he could lose everything.

d) ________ wanted to stop losing matches but he didn't know how to do it.

e) ________ had to act quickly to get evidence against ________.

Christiaans Tom Kate Sanchez

Chapter 13

New words 生词

- cheerfully /ˈtʃɪəfəli/ *ad.* 高兴地，愉快地
- digoxin /daɪˈgɒksɪn/ *n.* 地高辛，强心剂
- print-out /ˈprɪntaʊt/ *n.* 打印出的资料

Reading exercise 阅读练习

Complete the summary.

Raúl was going to ask Christiaans for more money so Kate would have recorded ________ for the police. The police had found some ________ called Lanoxin in Max's room. Lanoxin was a powerful ________ drug; perhaps it was used to kill Max. Kate picked up the computer ________ from Kanters; there was information about ________ against Rotterdam, made by the ________ ________. At ________ o'clock, someone knocked on Kate's door. Kate was expecting ________ and ________ but it was ________.

Chapter 14

New words 生词

- cellar /ˈselə(r)/ *n.* 地窖；地下室
- handcuff /ˈhændkʌf/ *v.* 给……戴上手铐
- multimillionaire /ˌmʌltimɪljəˈneə(r)/ *n.* 千万富豪
- unconscious /ʌnˈkɒnʃəs/ *a.* 无意识的，失去知觉的
- van /væn/ *n.* 厢式货车

Phrases & expressions 短语和表达

- if only ... 要是……就好了
- in position 在合适位置，就位
- knock somebody out 打晕某人
- know better than ... 很懂得而不至于……，明白事理而不至于……
- other than ... 除……之外
- there and then 当场，当时当地
- try out 尝试

Reading exercise 阅读练习

Put the events in the right order.

______ a) Kate ran to the central police station for help.

______ b) Raúl and Elly were now both safe.

______ c) Christiaans said Raúl would lose the game against Ajax.

______d) The police shot Christiaans in the leg.

______e) Kate knew she had to escape before the football match.

______f) Kate managed to get out of the cellar window.

______g) Elly and Kate were locked in a cellar.

Chapter 15

Phrases & expressions 短语和表达

- bring somebody back 使某人复活
- interview room 审讯室

Reading exercise 阅读练习

Match the questions and answers.

1) 'So he stabbed Max in his house?'

2) 'But why then stab him?'

3) 'And van Essen?'

4) 'And what about the rest of the Amsterdam Connection?'

5) 'But why did you let Christiaans take over the club?'

______a) 'Well, Christiaans had a body to get rid of somehow.'

______b) 'I didn't have any choice.'

______c) 'We're looking for them now, Miss Jensen.'

______d) 'Well, unfortunately he knew too much.'

______e) 'No ... Max was dead before he was knifed.'

Chapter 16

New word 生词

- cell /sel/ *n.* 牢房

Reading exercise 阅读练习

Who ...

a) had been a real friend to Kate?

b) was now in a police cell?

c) had put herself in danger to help Kate?

d) had been brave enough to do what was right?

e) had lost his brother?

f) had saved Kate's life long ago?

g) was pleased about Kate's story?

Translation
参考译文

幕后黑手

第 1 章　在酒吧

第5页

“你需要休假，凯特。”马克斯·卡森说。此时是黄昏时分，我们在女王之首酒吧喝啤酒。“暂时离开伦敦。”他补充说。

“哦，当然，马克斯，”我笑着说，“你去跟巴尔扎诺说吧，我相信他会同意的！”

戴夫·巴尔扎诺是一位非常优秀的报社主编，但是他经常对记者们发脾气。事实上，他的坏脾气是出了名的。我需要休假，巴尔扎诺就准我假，这样的想法很可笑。我和马克斯这样说。

“这么说来戴夫没变，对吧？”马克斯大笑着问。马克斯了解戴夫，也了解我，多年前我们都在《曼彻斯特晚报》工作。马克斯是主编，而戴夫是国外新闻部主管。马克斯给了我第一份工作。那时我只是个年轻的记者，努力想出名。那是在我来伦敦之前的事了。

“哦……没变，”我说，“他当然没变。”我笑着喝了一口啤酒。“不过说一说你的情况吧。”我接着说道。

第6页

我有一段时间没见马克斯了，主要是因为他现在住在荷兰。他出生在那儿。他的妈妈是荷兰人，爸爸是英国人。他在 20 岁刚出头时来到英国接受记者培训，并留了下来。但是五年前，马克斯 55 岁的时候从《曼彻斯特晚报》退休，回到了荷兰。

“我很好。”马克斯说。

“俱乐部呢？”我问。

马克斯的弟弟，汤姆，是鹿特丹城市足球俱乐部和卡森足球学校的老板兼经理。马克斯离开《曼彻斯特晚报》时，就已经加入他弟弟的俱乐部，帮他打理生意。马克斯现在持有大约 25% 的股份，还有一份不错的“退休”收入。

“还行。”马克斯说。

“只是还行？”我惊讶地问道。

“嗯……是的。”马克斯说。我感觉他并不太想谈论这件事，于是我换了话题。

近来马克斯不常来英国，除了来看朋友和为鹿特丹城市足球俱乐部寻找新球员。他来伦敦时，会到《每日回声报》的办公室来看我，我们常常去女王之首喝啤酒。这是一家典型的伦敦市中心的酒吧，里面坐满了办公室职员，个个拿着手机。晚上的这个时候，酒吧里烟雾缭绕，嘈杂不堪，但是这里的啤酒非常好喝。

第7页

“伦敦城里有什么事发生吗，凯特？”马克斯问。

马克斯总是问我最近的新闻，他想知道发生了什么事，他依然热爱新闻行业。他和巴尔扎诺完全相反，这不仅仅是因为巴尔扎诺的父亲是意大利人，而马克斯的母亲是荷兰人。巴尔扎诺是一位出色的主编，但是你永远不知道他什么时候会爆发。而马克斯冷静，很容易共事——他是最优秀的同事之一。

我给他讲了我的上一个新闻报道，以及我为什么这么疲惫不堪。

“你只是需要休息一下。”马克斯又说。

马克斯说得对，我的确需要休假。过去几个月，我在这座城市里的生活真的很难。我报道了几起难破的谋杀案，伦敦警方一如既往地无法提供任何信息，可巴尔扎诺还是像往常一样催我。我开始感到累了，离开伦敦的想法很有吸引力。

第8页

“你喜欢荷兰，不是吗？”马克斯突然问。

我笑着说：“噢，对，但是……”我去过一次阿姆斯特丹，追踪报道一起案件，我喜欢那个城市。

“而且你了解一些体育运动。”他补充说。

“噢，我了解空手道，也懂一点儿拳击，”我说，“对于其他运动就了解得没有那么多了。”我练过十年空手道，我爸爸年轻时是一名拳击手。

我看着马克斯，等待他下面要说的话。

“听着，”他说，“你为什么不来荷兰写一写我们的俱乐部呢？”

鹿特丹城市足球俱乐部现在是欧洲的顶尖俱乐部之一。许多在卡森足球学校受过训练的年轻人，都在鹿特丹城市足球队效力。俱乐部把会踢球的孩子从街上带走，训练他们成为最好的球员。像他们这样的足球学校是荷兰拥有如此多伟大足球运动员的原因之一。学校和俱乐部都很完美。

马克斯一直超喜欢足球。在《曼彻斯特晚报》当主编时，他把所有的业余时间都用来看足球比赛。他甚至带我去看过一次曼联。他是那种知道欧洲每一个足球运动员名字的人。

第9页

“什么？我？”我笑了，“一名体育记者？你知道我，马克斯，我只写犯罪案件。”

马克斯笑了。“我知道，凯特，你很棒。但是这对你来说算是一个假期！”

马克斯看了看表，快速把啤酒喝完。那天晚上，他约了一个朋友吃饭，不得不马上离开。他已经迟到了。他站了起来，答应过几天给我打电话。

但是他一直没给我打电话。事实上，我再也没见过他。两天后，他被发现死在了阿姆斯特丹的一条街上，身上有 20 处刀伤。

第 2 章　往事

第10页

“为什么会这样，里克？”我一遍又一遍地问我的同事，“这讲不通，完全没有道理！”

我和里克都是《每日回声报》的新闻记者。我们俩的办公桌紧挨着。我们每天一起工作，就像今天这样的时刻，我常和他说说心里话。我们是从伦敦警方那里获知了马克斯遇害的消息。

“可能只是个抢劫犯，凯特，想抢马克斯的钱。”里克温和地说。

“什么，在阿姆斯特丹？”我说。

阿姆斯特丹是世界上最安全的城市之一。软性毒品和色情的确有，但根本没太多的犯罪，当然更没有暴力犯罪了。大约两年前，在报道一个英国人在阿姆斯特丹卖偷来的画儿那起案件期间，我逐渐熟知了这个城市。那时，我还在荷兰警察中交了一个朋友。

警方是凌晨在阿姆斯特丹一个叫德派普的地方发现的马克斯的尸体。我知道荷兰警方会认为这是一起因抢劫而误杀致死的案件——一个醉汉或一个吸毒成瘾的人企图抢马克斯的钱。看起来马克斯好像进行了反抗，但是不幸的是，那个家伙手中有刀，变得丧心病狂了。

第11页

“但是马克斯怎么会大半夜在外面走动？”我问，“而且是在阿姆斯特丹——他不住在阿姆斯特丹。”

里克转过身来，视线离开了电脑屏幕，直视着我的双眼。

“这个嘛，你知道的，凯特……阿姆斯特丹的男人们……”他开始说。他没必要继续说下去。

阿姆斯特丹是欧洲的色情之都，这一点大家都知道。但是我无法想象马克斯会去阿姆斯特丹著名的红灯区。我不知道确切的原因，只是感觉这不像他，不是我认识的马克斯。

“马克斯？”我说，“我觉得不会。”

然而，我不得不承认里克说得没错。马克斯可能有任何理由去那里。毕竟，他住在荷兰。他凭什么告诉我他的计划？我们似乎也并不经常见面。我现在怀疑自己是否真的了解他。

第12页

我想了一会儿，然后说：“你知道吗，里克，有一些关于马克斯的事情，我从来没告诉过你。”

“什么事？”里克问。

“他救过我的命。”我说。

“救过你的命？”里克重复道，转过身来全神贯注地听我讲。

“是的，”我说，“我刚开始在《曼彻斯特晚报》当记者时，他们让我写有关婴儿和婚姻的报道。你知道的，就是那种平常的事情……”

里克微笑着点点头，他完全明白我的意思。他的第一份工作是在苏格兰的一个小镇，在那里他花了两年时间报道绵羊失窃。

“但是我真的很想写有关犯罪的报道，”我继续说，“你知道……我认为我当时真的太年轻、太笨了。我想报道一件大事——最大的。我希望能捕获一条真正的大鱼，让自己出名。”

“噢，那是自然。”里克说。

“是的，问题是那条大鱼是约翰尼·麦格劳，曼彻斯特最危险的罪犯之一。他真的不是只好鸟儿，就是那种会把人的脚上绑上重物扔进河里的家伙。”

第13页

“那发生了什么事？”里克问。

“马克斯让我报道一起简单的案件，一起发生在曼彻斯特市中心的入室抢劫案。住在房子里的人试图阻止这帮人偷他的东西。发生了打斗，那名男子重伤不治而死，所以这就变成了谋杀。有目击者目睹了案件的发生，但是没人能让他们开口讲这件事，即使是警方也无能为力。”

我喝了一口咖啡。“总之呢，”我继续说，“那些家伙是约翰尼·麦格劳团伙的成员，麦格劳会杀死任何出来说话的人。”

“你想办法让他们开口了？”里克问。

“你猜对了，”我说，“这是我获得真正大新闻的机会！但是约翰尼·麦格劳知道，这件事会牵连到他，他悬赏25,000英镑买我的人头。如果有人杀了我，麦格劳就会给他这笔钱。”

“随后发生了什么？”里克问，睁大了眼睛。

“你可以想象有很多人要杀我。我不得不向警方寻求保护一段时间，”我说，“警察一天 24 小时保护我。我的意思是事情真的很严重。然而过了一段时间，什么事也没发生。大约一个月之后，我不再躲藏，一切似乎都很好。但是后来麦格劳的人抓住了我。”

第14页

“但是你被放了？”里克问。

“是的，在马克斯的帮助下。马克斯知道我那天晚上要去哪儿。我失踪后，他出去找我了。他冒着生命危险来救我。最终，他和麦格劳达成协议，麦格劳就放了我。”我说。

我停了下来，想哭却哭不出来。

“总之，”我继续说，“马克斯救了我的命，我永远也不会忘记。”

“哇，凯特……很精彩的故事。”里克说。

“是啊，”我说，“我从来没告诉过你，我猜是因为我太蠢了。我讨厌谈论自己有多愚蠢。”

里克碰碰我的胳膊，笑了。

但那都是过去的事了，现在马克斯死了。在《每日回声报》有很多人认识马克斯，他们都觉得他的死令人难以置信：他死得那么突然、那么惨。对我来说，情况更糟糕，因为我近期刚见过他。我知道我必须去阿姆斯特丹，而且我也知道，如果我要去，我必须向我的主编——戴夫·巴尔扎诺——请假。

第15页

* * *

“你想去哪儿，詹森？”巴尔扎诺喊道。他身体肥胖，爱出汗，从来不会小声说话。

“阿姆斯特丹。”我说。

“为什么要这么做？”巴尔扎诺生气地问。“马克斯是被一个想要钱的瘾君子杀死的！”接着他停顿了一会儿。我能看出，巴尔扎诺对于马克斯的死感到悲伤。毕竟，马克斯曾经也是他的编辑。

我看着巴尔扎诺。“我想去，戴夫。”我轻声说。

巴尔扎诺知道马克斯对我来说很特别，他知道在曼彻斯特发生过的事。

“好吧，好吧，”他最后说，“你为什么不带上里克一起去？”

“不了，没有必要……真的。”我说。我不确定我会发现什么，如果有的话，但是我知道我必须去！而且我必须一个人去。我搭乘我能赶上的最早的航班。我要按照马克斯的意愿去阿姆斯特丹了——不是去报道他的俱乐部，而是去找出杀害他的凶手。

第 3 章　阿姆斯特丹的春天

第16页

我星期一上午 9:30 到达阿姆斯特丹。我在史基浦机场给埃莉·范普拉格打了个电话，她在荷兰警察局工作。埃莉是我在两年前报道偷画儿案件时结交的朋友。

那天上午埃莉没上班，我们约定两小时后在我们都熟悉的一家咖啡馆见面，在阿姆斯特丹的老城区约丹区。这样我就有时间去酒店登记入住了。我从机场搭乘火车，然后从中央火车站打了一辆出租车到市中心。报社给我订了皇帝运河边上的一个酒店。春天来阿姆斯特丹的游客很多，很难订到好房间。这家酒店条件不是很好，但我没打算在这儿待很久。我放下包就去见埃莉了。

我到的时候，埃莉已经在咖啡馆了，她坐在外面的一张桌子旁，旁边就是王子运河。看见我走来，她微笑着站了起来，以荷兰人的方式吻了我三次。“嘿，凯特，很高兴见到你。”她说。

第17页

埃莉是典型的荷兰人，如果有这样的说法的话。她个子很高，头发金黄，看起来像个运动员。事实上，她骑自行车骑得很好；当她不在阿姆斯特丹打击犯罪时，通常会在荷兰骑上数百千米的自行车，背上贴着个号码。她看起来像个荷兰农民的女儿，她确实是，面颊红润，眼睛又亮又蓝。和大多数与她年龄相仿的荷兰人一样——她 30 刚出头——她英语说得非常好。

我们坐下点了咖啡。这是一个明媚的春日，天空是蓝色的，四处漂浮着小块白云。

“关于你朋友的事，我很遗憾。”埃莉说。

“是的，”我盯着红白相间的桌布说，“的确令人伤心。”

我跟她说了几天前我和马克斯的会面。“他看起来很高兴，说俱乐部运转还行。”我补充道。

埃莉不是足球迷，对鹿特丹俱乐部一无所知。不过她确实了解阿姆斯特丹的犯罪案件。

第18页

德派普，马克斯死的地方，是阿姆斯特丹最老的街区之一，是一个非常热闹的地方，其中心地带有一个相当不错的街市，就在艾伯特大街上。上一次我来阿姆斯特丹，在那里买了荷兰奶酪和郁金香带回家。想到这个可爱又五彩缤纷的地方竟然是马克斯失去生命的地方，给人一种很奇怪的感觉。

“德派普地区近来变得非常危险，凯特，”埃莉说，“那里发生了很多持刀和枪击事件。我们最近一直在那儿忙。"

"这么说，这起案件看起来就像是抢劫引起的误杀？"我问。

服务员送来了咖啡，埃莉的是黑咖啡，我的是"错误的咖啡"——这是荷兰人对加了牛奶的咖啡的称呼。埃莉还点了一块蛋糕，打击犯罪和骑车运动使她饥肠辘辘。

"嗯。"埃莉说着，喝了口浓咖啡。"恐怕事情就是这样，凯特。他只是在错误的时间出现在了错误的地方。可怜的家伙，"她接着又说，"当然，我们会对他进行尸检。"

警方总是要求对这样的尸体进行尸检。想到马克斯躺着死去的样子，身上还有 20 处刀伤，我就感觉冷飕飕的，尽管春天的空气很暖和。

第19页

"那是谁发现的他？"我问。

"我们发现的。噢，是星期四深夜在城里巡逻的一队警察。"埃莉回答。

星期四，就是我在女王之首酒吧与马克斯见面的两天后。我眺望着运河。今天天气不错，很暖和，街道上和横跨运河的桥上到处都是人，有的骑车，有的步行。景色很美。很难想象马克斯死了，更难以想象他死在了阿姆斯特丹。这是一座如此可爱的城市。

"他当时住在史佩街上的郁金香客栈。"埃莉说。

我不知道这家宾馆，但是我知道史佩街就在老城区的中心。

"他们在他的尸体上根本没有找到多少线索。没什么特别的。"她说。

没什么特别的。人死后几乎是一样的。或许有一些钱，几张名片，也许还有几张家人的照片。只不过马克斯没有什么家人：他的妻子几年前就死了，他们没有孩子。他只有一个弟弟，汤姆。

第20页

“凶手拿走了他的钱吗？”我问。如果是抢劫，钱肯定是唯一的理由。

“嗯，警察没有找到他的钱包。”她说。

当然，这也说明不了什么，我想。如果有人想让这看上去像是抢劫，他们要做的第一件事情就是拿走钱。

“我们认为他很可能进行了反击，攻击他的人发疯了。这是常有的事。”埃莉说。

确实如此。

“他为什么在这儿过夜？”我问，“他为什么不直接回海牙去呢？坐火车只要40分钟左右。”

我知道马克斯住在海牙附近。他曾经几次邀请我去他家住，尽管我从来没去过。我好像总是没有时间。现在我再也没有机会了。

“他第二天上午一定有商务会议。很明显，他经常住在阿姆斯特丹，”埃莉说，“宾馆经理说，他以前在那儿住过。”

埃莉起身要去上班。

“谁负责马克斯的案子？”我问。

第21页

“乔普·德弗里斯，谋杀案侦破组。”她说。她的表情告诉我她不是很喜欢那个人。“噢，对了，”她边说边打开自行车的车锁，骑上了车，“马克斯的口袋里有一张卡片，上面写着一个名字和地址。我记下了。”她把手伸进外衣的口袋里拿出一张纸，上面写着什么。她把纸给了我。上面写着：“乔斯·范埃森，欧德斯堡141。”

我对足球了解不多，但是我知道这个名字。乔斯·范埃森是有史以来最伟大的球员之一。

第 4 章　与前锋交谈

第22页

我看着埃莉骑着车从桥上走了，她的蓝色夹克在身后随风飘动。

我坐回桌旁，思考着。乔斯·范埃森是一名伟大的球员，就像贝利、克鲁伊夫和希勒一样。他是一个真正的明星。他作为前锋为荷兰踢过很多次球，并且总是能进很多球。他长得也很英俊。报纸上总是刊载有关他女朋友的报道，她们通常是模特或演员。我记得最近在报纸上看到他退役了。人们感到很惊讶，因为他只有 28 岁，还挺年轻的，不到退役的年龄。

我拿出地图。欧德斯堡距此有很长一段路要走。我上次来阿姆斯特丹时去过那里，当时我去了比姆维斯爵士乐俱乐部。那里是该市很美的一个地方。今天天气很好，因此我决定走着去，可以边走边思考。我向欧德斯堡走去，去拜访这位前足球运动员。

我横穿运河时，一阵微风拂面，吹来一股咸味。在阿姆斯特丹，大海从不遥远。我拐进市政厅大街，朝达姆广场走去。看起来马克斯像是到阿姆斯特丹出差的。里克居然错误地以为他是来嫖娼的，想到这点我感到很欣慰。因为如果真是那样的话，就意味着马克斯一直很孤单，而我不想把他想象成一个孤独寂寞的老人。

第23页

这位退役的足球运动员住在欧德斯堡运河边的一幢公寓里，位于阿姆斯特丹最古老的一个城区。我到他公寓的时候已经下午 1:30

了。我按响了门铃，对讲机里传来了乔斯·范埃森的声音。我告诉他我是马克斯的朋友，门就开了。

“到顶楼来，詹森小姐。”他说。他的声音轻柔悦耳。

像所有荷兰的房子一样，这幢楼又高又窄，楼梯非常狭窄。我终于爬上了顶楼，叩响了门。我听见了范埃森开门的声音。开门花了一些时间——有三四道锁。随后他出现了，微笑着。他的笑容很帅气。

“爬上来不容易，对吧?”他说。他看起来和我在《每日回声报》体育版上看到的照片一模一样。他高高的个子，有着我曾见过的最漂亮的深棕色眼睛和最洁白的牙齿。他穿着黑色的牛仔裤和粉色的衬衣，在黝黑的皮肤衬托下，看起来特帅。他的身体看起来依然健硕。身材真棒！我开始喜欢上我的工作了。

第24页

“请进，詹森小姐。”他说，依然微笑着。他打开门，领着我进入他的公寓。

公寓不是很大，但是在荷兰公寓通常都很小。不过他肯定很有钱——家具看起来很昂贵。我记得在报纸上读过有关他的一些报道，当时他依然效力于鹿特丹队。新闻报道说他赚了几百万。我猜这只是他在市区的公寓。他可能在什么地方还有座大房子，或许在海边，或许在国外。

公寓虽然不大，但是位置非常好。它正对着运河，而且就在伦勃朗故居的附近。大大的落地窗开着，我能感觉到吹进屋内的暖风。在咖啡桌上有张鹿特丹城市足球队的照片，该队四年前赢得了欧洲杯，这张照片是让人知道公寓的主人是足球运动员的唯一标志。乔斯站在前排。马克斯和一个跟他长得很像但看起来比较年轻的人——我猜是汤姆——站在球队旁边，微笑着。

第25页

“啊，是的，美好的时光！”他看见我在欣赏照片时说道，“当时我们是最优秀的！”乔斯看起来有点儿伤感。

他让我坐在一把舒适的扶手椅上，然后说：“喝点儿咖啡吧，詹森小姐。我刚煮好了一壶。”他走进厨房，几乎是立刻就回来了，手里端着咖啡。

“这么说，你是体育记者，在写有关鹿特丹城市足球队的故事？”他边问边把咖啡壶放在低矮的玻璃桌上。

“是的，我想写写俱乐部的事情，”我说，“我想英国的足球迷对此会很感兴趣。”

我解释说，我在马克斯去世的前两天见过他。

“你是马克斯的朋友？”他说着给我倒了一杯咖啡。“真是太令人伤心了，太可怕了……发生这样的事真恐怖！我简直不敢相信。”

乔斯·范埃森看起来快要哭了，但是他忍住了。

“是的，太糟糕了，”我说，“而且让人难以理解。警方认为他是被一个抢劫犯杀害的。

“对，”乔斯忧心忡忡地说，“他们是这么认为的……”

第26页

有那么一会儿，我以为他要说更多的话，但是他什么也没说。

“那你很了解马克斯了？”我继续说道。

“噢，是的，我很了解他。他来俱乐部后，真的帮了我，真的帮我成了一名伟大的足球运动员。”

他伸手去拿咖啡杯。我再次觉得他在努力忍着不哭。然后他继续说了下去。

“鹿特丹城市足球俱乐部对我很好。”他再次看着照片说，“汤姆·卡森发现我时，我才十岁，生活在一个儿童教养所。你知道这个故事的，很有名。汤姆来看我踢球，他在我身上看到了别人都看不到的东西。他把我带到卡森足球学校，让我接受良好的教育，养活我，让我踢球。在学校里，他们训练我如何真正地踢球……是他们第一次送了我一双足球鞋。”

他笑了。“我还留着我的第一双足球鞋，”他接着说，“在那之前，我只穿旧运动鞋踢球。他们给了我成为一个真正优秀的人的机会。这是我有生以来第一次感到幸福。”

乔斯看了看我，深吸了一口气。

“然后马克斯给了我实实在在的帮助，使我成了最棒的球员。”他说，“他来俱乐部时，我是一名不错的球员。但是马克斯和我谈话，帮助我，给了我为荷兰队踢球、成为伟大球员所需要的一切……他很伟大，是一个伟大的人。”

第27页

乔斯·范埃森曾效力于荷兰队，是赢得世界杯的足球队的一员。

“我并不太知道马克斯在俱乐部做什么工作。”我说，“难道汤姆不是教练、总经理吗?”

“是的，没错，”乔斯说，“马克斯是一名球探，他帮助汤姆到荷兰各地以及欧洲的其他地方为俱乐部寻找优秀的年轻球员，也为足球学校寻找有踢球潜质的孩子。”

“而且他似乎很擅长这项工作。”我说。

“他是最棒的。”乔斯说。

马克斯一直很活跃，即使退休了，他依然喜欢旅行和工作。我还记得马克斯总是知道一个年轻的球员什么时候能成为伟大的球员。

“马克斯和他弟弟亲近吗？他们的关系好吗？”我问。

乔斯看起来有点儿不自在。“好……”他慢慢回答，“虽然他们最近一直在争吵。”

“争吵什么？”

第28页

“我不知道，”乔斯说着移开了目光。我有一种感觉，他知道的比他说的要多。

“马克斯的尸体被发现时，他身上为什么带着你的名片？”我问。如果乔斯和马克斯非常熟悉，他为什么还需要名片？

“我刚刚搬到这儿，这是我的新公寓。”范埃森笑着在房间里挥手解释道，“我星期四晚上去见了马克斯，给了他我的新地址，就这些。”

“你星期四见他了？”我问。

就在那天晚上，马克斯被发现死在了德派普。

“是的，”他说，“我告诉警察了。星期四晚上，挺早的，大约7:00。我们俩一起在绅士运河边的德贝雅德酒吧喝酒。我们俩都在市里时，常常在那儿见面，只是聊聊天，喝杯啤酒。”他笑着补充说：“他们那儿的啤酒种类特别多。”

“然后呢？”我问。

“我不知道他具体做了什么，”乔斯说，“我当时有一个饭局，他说他要去见一个人。”

“他说要去见谁了吗？”我问。

“没有。”

“他是走着去的吗？”我又问。

第29页

“不是。他说他要打车去。”乔斯回答说。

“这么说，他要见的人不住在市中心。”我说。

“我不确定，”乔斯说，“即使距离很近，马克斯也经常打车。由于他的心脏不好，他不喜欢太累。”

“他的心脏？”我问。

“是的，马克斯的心脏不好。他患过心脏病……哦，我想大约是四年前。”乔斯说。

关于马克斯的这一情况我并不了解。

“那他吃药吗？”

“吃，我想是这样……对，我确定。我见他吃过好几次。”乔斯回答。

“马克斯告诉我俱乐部里有一些问题。”我撒谎说。

乔斯看起来有点儿惊讶。

“哦……是的。我不知道，我真的什么都不知道。我大约一年前就离开了，”他说，“我不知道现在发生了什么。”他把视线从我身上移开。

“你们没有谈论这个吗？”我问。

“没有，我们没谈。”乔斯说。他说话的口气听起来好像没有什么好说的了。

第30页

“你从球场上退役是怎么回事？你为什么28岁就退役了？”我问，“这个年龄还很年轻。”

“哦，你知道的，我想干点儿别的，”他说，依然看着别处，“我还不确定做什么，但是，不再踢足球了。我还年轻，但我已经踢球很长时间了，詹森小姐。”

我喝完咖啡，站起来要走。

“我住在皇帝运河边上的洲际酒店。”临走时我说。

乔斯·范埃森打开四道门锁，和我道了别。

第 5 章　在斯劳泽餐厅的晚餐

第31页

按响范埃森家的门铃一小时之后，我又回到了欧德斯堡，看着运河上的船只，看着河面上舞动的灯光。

我看了看地图，不知道该怎么办。或许我应该去德派普，那是马克斯的尸体被发现的地方。

德派普在阿姆斯特丹的另一头，因此我在温暖的阳光里走了一小会儿，然后坐上了有轨电车。我到了那里后，在街上走了一会儿，而后穿过了市场。这是一个有趣的、色彩缤纷的地方。你可以在这里买到任何东西：新鲜的果蔬、肉、鸡蛋、奶酪和鲜花。当然了，荷兰以郁金香闻名，这里的郁金香非常漂亮。

我穿过那条埃莉告诉我他们发现马克斯尸体的街道。它的一头是一条更大的街道，另一头是一个叫萨帕提的公园。埃莉说过，就是公园周边的区域正变得越来越危险。街道的一侧只有一座公寓楼。即使在阳光下，它看起来也是灰暗、悲伤的。

第32页

警察在马克斯死的地方围了一圈绳子，不让人们靠近。我看着那个地方，感觉到一股寒意。我走进市场一角的一家小咖啡馆兼酒吧，坐在吧台点了杯茶暖和一下身子。

酒吧里面只有几个顾客，大多是看起来在市场里工作的男人。酒吧老板是一个非常友善的人，他大腹便便，脸色红润。他开始和我聊天。他的英语说得非常好。我们聊这聊那，然后我说：“我听说前几天晚上这里发生了一起凶杀案。”

“噢，是的，”酒吧老板说，“大麻烦。警察几乎一直都在这儿。”

“这附近经常发生这种事吗？”我问。

“嗯，情况越来越糟糕了。”他说。

“这个地区发生的事情太可怕了。”我身边的一个声音说。

我转过身来。坐在我旁边的是一位老人，他一边喝着荷兰杜松子酒，一边吸着烟。他个子不高，肤色黝黑，好像一辈子都在室外工作。他头发稀疏，当他朝我微笑时，我注意到他只有几颗深棕色的牙齿。

“我叫伯特。”他说着伸出了手。

第33页

伯特喜欢聊天。他问我从哪里来，我们谈起了伦敦，他 20 年前去过那里。我们闲聊了一会儿，然后话题又回到了谋杀案上。

“这里所有的人都听说过这件事，”他说，“案发现场离这儿仅隔着两条街。”他喝了一口杜松子酒。“是的，好多天了，那里到处都是警察。”伯特的脸看上去很悲伤。“太糟糕了……太糟糕了。”我不知道是这起暴力犯罪，还是在德派普有如此多的警察让伯特觉得太糟糕了。

我喝茶时，我们又多聊了几句，之后我起身要走。“如果你听到了与案件有关的事情，给我打电话。我是死者家人的朋友。”我说谎道。我给了伯特一张纸条，上面写着我的电话号码和我所住酒店的名字。我离开酒吧时，他正凝视着那张纸条。

我返回酒店，回到房间，躺在床上，脑海里浮现出一些疑问：为什么马克斯那么想让我写有关俱乐部的事？只是因为他觉得我需要休假吗？乔斯·范埃森为什么那么害怕？我把一盒约翰·柯川的磁带放进随身听里，听一些世上最好听的爵士萨克斯管音乐。

第34页

床头柜上的电话一直在我耳边响，我被吵醒了。过了片刻我才意识到自己睡着了，又过了一会儿才意识到自己在哪里。我还戴着耳机，虽然磁带已经停了。我摇摇头使自己清醒过来，摘掉耳机。是埃莉的电话。

“呃……埃莉，怎么了？”因为刚睡醒，大脑依然糊里糊涂，我不知道几点了。不过天已经黑了。

“凯特，你在睡觉吗？”她问。

“哦，我刚才睡着了。几点了？”我问，清醒了一些。

“7:00了，我刚下班。凯特，咱们见面喝一杯吧。”她说。

半个小时后，我们坐进了酒店附近的一家酒吧喝啤酒。我告诉了埃莉我和范埃森见面的情况，以及我去德派普的走访。

“你很幸运！”她笑着说，“大多数女人为了能有机会跟范埃森说句话甘愿去死。”

“哦，大多数时间我都在采访丑陋的罪犯，”我笑着说，“跟一个长得帅的人谈话感觉挺棒的。”

“你有什么有趣的发现吗？”

“没有什么，”我说，“但是我有一种感觉，他在害怕什么事情……或者什么人。他的公寓锁得像银行一样严严实实的！”

第35页

埃莉大笑。

“我要去给巴尔扎诺打个电话，”我说着朝吧台另一端的电话走去。我没有太多话和他讲，但是让他保持冷静总是个好主意。

“不，等一等，”她说着抓住我的胳膊，“等到晚饭后再打吧。我有话跟你说。”

我们决定去位于乌特勒支大街上的斯劳泽餐馆吃晚饭，于是就打车去了那里。在阿姆斯特丹，这里是我最喜欢的餐馆之一。这里实际上是两家餐馆，鱼餐馆和肉餐馆，它们都非常棒。餐馆内到处挂着漂亮的老式镜子，服务员穿着黑色的西装，系着白色的围裙。而且食物总是做得非常好，你选择哪个餐馆都行。今晚我们选择的是肉餐馆。我们坐下，点了牛排和一瓶波尔多葡萄酒。忙了一天，我感到很饿。

突然埃莉用一种很特别的眼神看着我，当她有重要事情要说时，就会这样看着我。我能从餐桌旁边的大镜子里看见她严肃的脸。“凯特，有件事情我得告诉你。”她说。

“嗯？”我嚼了一块牛排说。

第36页

“他们认为今天找到了杀害马克斯的凶手。”她说。

我放下了刀叉。“他们？”我问。

“德弗里斯的人。他们抓了一个人。他们相当确定是他干的。”

“但是这个家伙承认了吗——说他杀了马克斯？”我问。

“没有，”她说，“我想没有，但是他们在他的公寓里发现了马克斯的钱包。他们现在正在找那把刀。”

“那人是谁？”我问。

“一个住在那个区的家伙，”她说，“一个当地出了名的瘾君子和抢劫犯。”

那么事情就是这样了，我想。看起来大家都是对的。马克斯的谋杀案是一起没有意义的杀人案，凶手是一个需要钱买毒品的变态的家伙。我双手抱着头——我感觉有些不舒服。

“我很抱歉，凯特。”埃莉补充说。

我一时说不出话来。然后，突然，我想起了那天晚上马克斯和我在女王之首酒吧说的话。“你需要休假。”他当时说，“来写一写俱乐部的事吧。”马克斯到底为什么要我报道鹿特丹城市足球俱乐部呢？

“我不相信。”我抬起头说。这句话甚至对我来说都令人吃惊。

第37页

我猜想阿姆斯特丹警方想尽快抓住凶手。如果凶手是当地一个令他们讨厌的罪犯，这对他们来说比较容易。他们和其他地方的警察并无区别。

“但是凯特……”埃莉开始说。

“我不知道为什么，但这件事有点儿不对劲。”我几乎是大声喊着说。坐在我们旁边的一对中年夫妇看向我。我在流汗，依然感到不舒服。我说话的声音低了些。“还有其他事情……”

埃莉和蔼地朝我笑着说：“瞧，凯特，我只是告诉你。我根本没有调查这起谋杀案。”我知道这是事实。埃莉正在城市另一边调查另外一起案件。

“我知道，埃莉，谢谢，”我说，“但是我就是有一种感觉……”

她又笑了。“我不知道真相是什么，”她继续说道，“但是我想我最好告诉你。明天德弗里斯就会在报纸和电视上宣布这件事，全世界的人就都知道了。”

我知道埃莉认为我对马克斯的感情是如此强烈，以至于我不能接受他的死，不能接受他死的方式。我自己也开始疑惑起来。一个救过你命的人死了，你很难接受，也很难看清事实的真相。我想知道巴尔扎诺的想法。

第38页

巴尔扎诺！我突然想起来我得给他打个电话。我赶紧喝了半杯酒壮胆，跑到了大厅里的电话边。

“詹森！”巴尔扎诺尖叫道。我把电话听筒从耳边拿开了一小会儿。巴尔扎诺有些不开心，他不开心时，从不打招呼。

“终于打电话了！我以为你消失了。”他大声说。消失！我只在阿姆斯特丹待了一天。

“听着，”他继续说，“今天晚上《公报》上有一篇关于马克斯的报道，是乔·西蒙斯写的。”巴尔扎诺从牙缝里挤出这个名字。《公报》是伦敦另外一家大型报纸，而乔·西蒙斯是他们最优秀的记者。

“什么……乔·西蒙斯说了什么？”我问。

“说他们找到了杀害马克斯的凶手，”巴尔扎诺接着说，“一切都结束了。你到底在阿姆斯特丹跑来跑去干什么……我付钱给你是为了什么，詹森？”

即使电话听筒远离我的耳朵，我也能清楚地听到巴尔扎诺说的话。

这是个坏消息。不知怎么，西蒙斯抢先得到了信息，而让巴尔扎诺真正生气的一件事就是《公报》先于我们得到消息。哦，对此我也不高兴。

第39页

巴尔扎诺停了几秒钟喘口气，我及时插话了。

“戴夫，听我说，这不是真的……至少我不这么认为。”我说，希望我是对的。

“不是真的?”巴尔扎诺尖声喊道，“岂有此理，詹森。他们发现了马克斯的钱包！那个家伙拿着他的钱包！你还想要什么?”

“我不知道，戴夫，”我说，“我只是有一种感觉，还有别的情况。给我点儿时间。”

我放下电话。

“怎么样?”埃莉问，我返回时她几乎吃完了她的牛排。骑着自行车跑来跑去无疑让她饥肠辘辘了。

“坏消息，”我说，“你说的消息已经出来了，不管是不是真的，巴尔扎诺很不开心。当我说我需要时间的时候，他差一点儿心脏病发作。但是他最终还是同意了。”埃莉大笑起来。她从来没见过巴尔扎诺，但是她理解。

巴尔扎诺给了我三天时间，要么写篇报道，要么离开阿姆斯特丹。我把我那已经凉了的牛排向身前拉了拉。我有一种感觉，我将需要我所有的力量。

第 6 章　伯特提供的信息

第40页

回到酒店后，我收到了伯特留下的信息，就是我在德派普区的酒吧里遇见的那个老家伙。他留下了一个电话号码。虽然很晚了，但我还是从我的房间给他打了电话。伯特还在我几个小时前离开的那家酒吧里——我能听到他身后人们的谈话声和玻璃杯的声音。我不知道他是不是把所有时间都花在了那里。

“我有一些消息要告诉你，”他说，“一些非常有用的信息。但是我需要一些东西。”

“一些东西？”我问。

“一些钱，”他低声说，“400 荷兰盾。”400 荷兰盾，这可是 100 多英镑。如果他提供的信息没用，这么多钱就白花了，但是我只能同意。巴尔扎诺已经变得非常不耐烦，可我仍然一无所获。

“好的，伯特，没问题，”我说，“你现在能来我住的酒店吗？”

伯特 11:30 到了酒店，看上去比我离开他时更醉了。我们去了酒吧，他点了杜松子酒，我付的钱。我已经把 400 荷兰盾装进了一个信封里，现在我把它放在桌子上，用手压着。

第41页

“好了，伯特，”我说，“什么信息？”

他环视了一下房间，好像预料到有人在听似的。然后他看了看信封，喝了一口酒。

“我认识一个人，”他低声说，“他看到了星期三晚上（注：这里应该是伯特醉酒后记错了时间。）你朋友身上发生的事。他说你朋友被带到那条街上时就已经死了。有人把他从车里拖出来，然后捅了他好多刀。但是他已经死了，他之前就死了。他非常确定。”

伯特看了看我手底下的信封。我的手没有动。“这个人为什么不和警察说呢？”我问。

伯特大笑。“噢，他不喜欢警察，你知道的。他什么都不会告诉警察的。”好吧，有可能。有很多人不喜欢警察，尤其是他们是罪犯时。

“那他当时在哪儿，你说的这个人？”我问。

“他正从楼上的一扇窗户往外看。”伯特说，“有什么声音把他吵醒了。他没有开灯，只是来到窗边。他能看到一切。”

我不知道伯特说的是不是真话。我猜，更有可能的是这个人当时非法闯入了一座房子，所以他不能告诉警察。我想伯特应该会有这样的朋友。或者那个人甚至就是伯特自己？

第42页

“和我朋友在一起的是男的还是女的？”我问。

“男的，我朋友猜的，当时天很黑。”伯特说。

“车呢，是什么样的车？”我问。

伯特想了想。他不知道。天太黑了，而且车还停在了街的另一头。

“我以为他什么都能看到呢。”我说。

“哦，你知道的，几乎能看到一切，”伯特说，“他看见有人用刀捅他，这是肯定的。”

“那把刀呢？”我问，“那把刀在哪儿呢？”

伯特只是摇着头。“谁知道呢？”他说。

“听着，伯特，”我说，“我知道警察已经抓到了一个人。他们说他们在那个人的公寓里发现了我朋友的钱包。”

“我知道，我知道，”伯特不耐烦地说，“但这不是真的。他们抓的那个人——科尔·沙普——他不可能杀人，那条街上的人都知道这一点。他之前从没杀过人。现在怎么会开始杀人呢？”

第43页

“总会有第一次的。”我说。

“不会，不会，”伯特说，“他只不过是从尸体上偷走了钱包。大家都是这么认为的……所有人，除了警察。”

好吧，我想，也有可能。

第44页

我把信封给了伯特。他迅速拿起信封，喝完了酒，几乎是拿着钱跑了出去。我不知道他给我的信息是否是真的。或许伯特只是看到了轻松赚钱的机会。对我来说，这可能是昂贵的 100 英镑。

我回到自己的房间，躺在床上，看着昨天晚上鹿特丹足球俱乐部和莱顿队比赛的报道。报道刊登在荷兰的一家报纸《誓言报》上。我不懂荷兰语，但是我知道鹿特丹队 0∶2 输给了莱顿队。鹿特丹队踢得太差了。

我想知道鹿特丹城市足球俱乐部的经理汤姆·卡森对这场比赛有什么看法。

第 7 章　鹿特丹之行

第45页

阿姆斯特丹中央火车站是一座非常漂亮的建筑，但是我没有很多时间去欣赏它。我与汤姆·卡森约好星期二上午 10:00 在鹿特丹城市足球俱乐部的办公室见面。我到车站时已经快 8:30 了，我买了一张票，还买了杯咖啡和一个羊角面包，然后上了车。

荷兰是个很小的国家，所有的城镇彼此离得很近。到鹿特丹仅需一个多小时，所以我靠在座位上欣赏窗外的风景。平坦的绿色田野，花卉农场和奶牛，当然还有水。在荷兰，到处都有水。

我很难不去想马克斯的死。昨天晚上埃莉离开我之前，她警告我不要卷入案件太深。但是，我已经卷入其中了。就在几天前马克斯和我在女王之首酒吧聊天时，我就卷入了这件事。我参与其中是因为马克斯死了，我参与其中是因为他救过我的命，我欠他的。

当我望向窗外的荷兰乡村时，我想起了昨晚读到的关于鹿特丹队和莱顿队之间的比赛。我对足球了解不多，但我知道必须进球才能赢。我猜汤姆·卡森不会高兴的。但是还有比足球更重要的事情——这个人刚刚失去自己的哥哥。

第46页

火车很快到了鹿特丹站。鹿特丹和阿姆斯特丹很不一样，你坐火车一到站就能看到不同之处。鹿特丹和其他现代化城市一样，有着高大的玻璃建筑和公寓楼。它没有一点儿阿姆斯特丹的美，没有可爱的古建筑和运河。

我在俱乐部的办公室见到了汤姆·卡森。他很瘦，头发花白，50岁左右，和马克斯长得很像，我突然感到很伤心。汤姆有着运动员的健壮身体。他年轻时曾在阿贾克斯足球俱乐部踢球，他看起来像是依然能在球场上踢球。

“您能见我真是太好了，”我说，“马克斯的事我很难过。”

“是的，这事太可怕了，”汤姆·卡森说，“真是令人难以置信。根本没有道理。”马克斯的弟弟摇了摇头。他看上去很疲惫。

第47页

“马克斯是个非常优秀的人。”我说。

我们聊了聊马克斯和我们在曼彻斯特一起度过的时光。然后汤姆·卡森问道：“我能为你做一些什么，詹森小姐？”

“哦，我想写一篇关于荷兰的足球俱乐部的报道，和英国的俱乐部比较一下，”我解释道，“你知道的，训练啊——诸如此类的事情。鹿特丹城市足球俱乐部似乎是个很好的选择，不过也许现在时机不太好……”

我没告诉卡森是马克斯想让我来写有关俱乐部的报道。

“不，没关系，”他说，“生活还得继续。我们必须考虑俱乐部的未来。再过几分钟，那些小伙子们就要开始训练了。”

虽然汤姆·卡森对哥哥的死感到悲伤，但他不想错过这个为俱乐部做宣传的好机会。我想他是个优秀的商人。

我们出了办公室来到训练场，坐在场地边。“小伙子们”开始从办公室楼下的更衣室里出来。

“他们现在正在为欧洲杯的一场比赛做准备。明天晚上他们将在主场迎战巴塞罗那队。”他解释道。

第48页

我想知道他们在惨败给莱顿队之后将如何迎战巴塞罗那队。巴塞罗那队是欧洲最强的足球队之一。如果他们赢不了莱顿队，他们还有什么希望能赢“巴萨”？

“我想他们能行。”卡森说，仿佛看出了我的心思。但是我感觉他并不是真的相信自己的话。

球员们正在场外做热身运动。阳光灿烂，微风习习，和往日的荷兰一样。我们谈论着训练，我又多看了会儿球队，希望卡森不会意识到我对足球知之甚少。

“有意思的是，”卡森说，“学校和足球队——两者都有，这使得我们与众不同。”

“是的，听起来很有趣。”我说，“如果可能，我真的想去参观一下学校。”

卡森笑了。“那再容易不过了，詹森小姐。顺着路往下走就到了。我亲自带你去。”他说。临走前，我又看了一眼场上的球队。球员们在练习把球传给前锋，然后前锋射门。前锋们都很强，多数情况下都能把球踢进球门。

第49页

“他们看起来不错，”我对汤姆·卡森说，“我猜你希望明天晚上能进几个球吧。”

卡森忧虑地笑了一下。

汤姆·卡森带着我参观了卡森足球学校。男孩子们住在学校里。他们在那里睡觉、吃饭、学习、踢球。学校既现代又干净，有很好的教学和足球训练，汤姆说是“一流的”。孩子们到处都是，有的在学习，有的在踢球。他们年龄都很小，我猜在八到十五岁之间，不过有两三个年龄稍大的。

我们观看十个孩子进行某项训练时，汤姆说：“他们当中很多人来自非常贫困的家庭，詹森小姐。”他们踢着球，绕过排成一列的一些箱子，然后跑到终点射门。他们看起来不错，我想。优秀的运动员在某些方面是相同的，不管他们是练空手道、打网球还是踢足球。他们有很好的平衡能力，能保持头部不动。

“有几个孩子是荷兰人，但也有些来自南美洲和非洲。我们发现真正优秀的小男孩儿就把他们带到这里。”他继续说。

第50页

“那就是马克斯做的工作吗？”我问。

“是的，”他说，“马克斯寻找像这样的孩子，也寻找在其他球队踢球的优秀球员。”

我为我的“报道”做了一些笔记，又向四周看了看。孩子们无疑看起来很幸福，也得到了很好的照顾。

“他们当中大多数人能成为职业足球运动员吗？”我问。

“大多数能，”他说，“如果他们足够优秀的话。”

我和汤姆·卡森离开了学校。我握了握他的手，说了声再见，然后返回鹿特丹火车站。在回阿姆斯特丹的火车上，我很难不去想经理那悲伤的微笑。卡森不开心，我想，不仅仅是因为他刚刚失去了自己的哥哥。

第8章　扑朔迷离

第51页

回到阿姆斯特丹，我去了最大的公共图书馆——我要做一些调查工作。是时候查明谁是鹿特丹城市足球俱乐部真正的有钱人了。马克斯曾经告诉我，他持有俱乐部25%的股份，但是俱乐部只属于卡森兄弟吗？

图书管理员把我领到一台能上网的电脑前，然后我就开始工作了。我搜索了过去五六年中与鹿特丹城市足球俱乐部相关的信息。两个小时之后，我开始对俱乐部发生的事情有了一个大致的了解。

读到的内容很有意思。在过去的两年里，汤姆·卡森在俱乐部的股份从75%降到30%。但是汤姆的股份并没有给马克斯。马克斯在俱乐部的整个时间里，他的股份一直是25%。大部分股份都给了一个名叫马丁·克里斯蒂亚安斯的人。我回顾了过去几年的情况。克里斯蒂亚安斯两年前开始购买股份，最初只有10%，但是他现在持有鹿特丹城市足球俱乐部45%的股份。

第52页

我想知道马丁·克里斯蒂亚安斯是谁，汤姆·卡森为什么会允许他购买自己俱乐部的股份？

我不知道马克斯的股份现在怎么样了。毫无疑问，它们会直接留给汤姆·卡森。马克斯死了，他的弟弟现在拥有俱乐部55%的股份——在俱乐部处于十分有利的位置。

我离开公共图书馆。是时候做更多的调查了。

我从酒店房间内的电话号码簿入手。很幸运，我在里面只发现了一个名叫马丁·克里斯蒂亚安斯的人，地址在绅士运河。我想去看一看。

绅士运河距酒店步行只有五分钟的路程。我边走边想了一个和克里斯蒂亚安斯谈话的理由，如果他在家的话。我会说我在写有关阿姆斯特丹古建筑的报道，想和他谈一谈他住的房子。我知道绅士运河边到处都是漂亮的老房子。我来到了141号，抬头看着房子的顶部，仿佛突然对古建筑产生了兴趣。房子很美，大概是17世纪的建筑，保存得很好。很明显，克里斯蒂亚安斯极为富有。

第53页

我深吸了一口气，走上台阶，来到门口。门是用漂亮的黑檀木做的，主人名字上方有一个银色的门铃。我按响门铃，等了一下，然后又按了一次。家里没有人。

就在我转身要走时，一个大约25岁的年轻女子来到了隔壁，手里提着购物袋。她用荷兰语对我说了些什么，于是我说："抱歉，我听不懂。"

"哦，对不起，"那名女子朝我微笑着说，"我说如果你是在找克里斯蒂亚安斯先生的话，我看见他今天一早就出去了。"

“你知道他是做什么工作的吗？”我问。

“我不太确定。我不是很了解他。”说着，她打开自家门进了屋。

我似乎错过了克里斯蒂亚安斯，于是我返回了酒店。在酒店，我运气较好。在前台有我一封信。信是昨天从本市寄出的，是第二批送达的。信封上的地址和名字是打印的。信封上只写着“詹森小姐”，然后是酒店的名字和地址。我打开信封，里面有一张简短的便条，是用大写字母手写的：

第54页

亲爱的詹森小姐：

你应该调查一下赌莱顿队赢阿姆斯特丹队的那笔钱。

一个朋友

我不知道信是谁写的，但是这个人不会拼写“朋友”这个单词。（注：原文中“朋友”的拼写为FREIND，是错误拼写。）

“好消息？”前台的年轻女子问道。

“或许是……”我说。

赌莱顿队获胜的人是谁呢？我从哪儿可以查到？我打电话给埃莉。

“让我想想，”埃莉说，“大多数体育博彩都是通过一个名叫坎特斯的博彩公司进行的。试试去找他们在阿姆斯特丹这儿的办公室里一个叫罗尼的人，告诉他我的名字。他欠我的人情。他应该能帮你。”然后她补充道：“小心点儿，凯特。”

和埃莉谈完话几分钟之后，我给乔斯·范埃森打了电话。

“詹森小姐，真是个惊喜！”他说。

“范埃森先生，”我说，“我在想……我听说鹿特丹队明天要和巴塞罗那队比赛，我想去看比赛。”我知道作为一名退役球员，他肯定有票。

第55页

“噢……是的，当然。你为什么不和我一起去呢？”他问。

“那太好了！”我说。

“好的。我大约5:30开车到你住的酒店去接你。比赛7:30开始。晚安。”这位帅气的前锋说。

我放下电话。我想，生活开始变得有意思了。

* * *

那天晚上，生活突然变得更加有意思了。大约10:30的时候，我决定到外面散散步。我需要呼吸新鲜空气，也需要思考。这时天已经黑了，酒店附近走动的人很少。我沿着皇帝运河慢慢走着，眼睛盯着人行道，思考着白天发生的一切。我沿着运河一直走。

突然，一辆汽车在我身旁停了下来。一个黑影跳下车，走到我身后，把我的一条胳膊拉到背后。疼得要命。“上车，别出声，否则我弄断你的胳膊。”那家伙说。我没听出那个声音。

我抬起脚狠狠地踢了那家伙的右腿。同时，我抽回另外一条没被控制的胳膊，用肘部击打他的胸部。那家伙没有料到这个，很见效，他惊诧不已。

第56页

那家伙松开了手，我迅速转过身来。我抬起头，看见一个身材高大的黑发男子，长着一双明亮的蓝眼睛。

“过来吧。”他说。他拉我，想把我拉进车里。

“嘿，说请，”我边说边反抗。他笑了，几乎是在取笑我。这真的激怒了我。他很强壮，比我高大得多，但是我练过几年空手道，身手敏捷。我也知道如何突袭他。

他把我拉到靠近汽车的地方。我左脚后退一步，迅速抬起右腿，右脚在他的肚子上踢了一脚。我使出全身的力气来踢他，他大吃一惊。他的确身材高大，但是如果你击中腹部，块头大也没有优势。他开始像一棵树一样倒下。就在他倒下时，我又用肘部打了他的头。肘部是人身上骨头最硬的部分，很快他就双膝跪在地上，双手抱着头。此时他意识到，绑架我不是他想象的那么容易。他没想到我会这样反抗。他迅速爬进汽车，紧张地环顾四周。他很可能是害怕打斗的声音会引来人们围观。

第58页

他要逃跑。我扫视四周，想看看是否有人能帮我。但是街上空荡荡的。我想阻止他，但我一个人阻止不了他。紧接着我听到了一声刺耳的声音，袭击我的那个家伙发动了车子。他猛踩油门，沿路飞奔而去。

第 9 章　阿姆斯特丹联盟

第59页

我跑上楼回到自己的房间，锁好门，大口喘着气。我猜那家伙早就在酒店的外面监视我，等待机会了。我从房间的小冰柜里拿出一瓶威士忌，很快喝完了。我上床睡觉，但是睡得很不好。

第二天我打算去见罗尼，埃莉在坎特斯工作的那个“朋友”。但在我离开酒店房间之前，我又得到一个惊喜。埃莉在上班的路上来到我入住的酒店。阿姆斯特丹警方拿到了马克斯的尸检报告。她的一个朋友——德弗里斯的部下——告诉了她这件事。

“他们说他肯定是死于刀伤，”她说，“他失血过多。有 95% 的可能性他就是死在了德派普那里。”

“那他们依然认为凶手就是那个叫沙普的家伙？”我问。

“是的，”她说，“尽管他们还没有找到那把刀。”

第60页

我把伯特告诉我的事情说给埃莉听。埃莉只是看着我。她不必说什么。我们俩都知道伯特说谎的可能性更大，他只是为了得到钱。

“死亡时间呢？”我问她。

“他们还不能完全确定，但是大概在午夜到凌晨3:30之间。”埃莉说。

我没有把前一天晚上发生的事告诉埃莉。她去上班了，而我去了坎特斯。在酒店外面，我环顾四周，然后拦了一辆出租车。从现在起，我必须小心行事。

在坎特斯的办公室，我要求见罗尼。一位年轻的女士带我来到后面的一间办公室，罗尼正在电脑前工作。我进来时，他只是继续盯着电脑，几乎没看我一眼。办公室里很暗，只有后面有一扇小窗户。罗尼大约40岁，身材瘦小，几乎没有头发。他皮肤苍白，看起来很不健康。我猜他大多数时间都在这间阴暗的房间里工作。我解释了我想要什么。

“我不能给你提供这种信息。”他说，头都没抬。

第61页

我说了埃莉的名字。这很有效果。他转过身来，上下打量了我一下，然后关上门，这样前面办公室的人就听不到我们的谈话了。我不知道他欠了埃莉什么，但是很明显这个人情很大。

“一小时之后再来。”他低声说。

我来到外面，买了一份报纸，然后进了一家咖啡馆。我看了看体育版。有一篇关于今天晚上比赛的报道，我把能看懂的都看了。我望着窗外，喝着咖啡，思考着。

如果马克斯是在其他地方被刺的，就像伯特说的那样，那血迹呢？车上会有血，到处都会是血。这意味着一辆沾满血的车子被遗弃在了某个地方，或者一场大清理。

我回去见罗尼，现在他的电脑屏幕上已经显示着我需要的信息。我之前告诉他我在找一个大赌注，一大笔钱赌莱顿队赢鹿特丹队。

“大家都期望鹿特丹队会赢。”罗尼说。“他们是大家最喜欢的球队。赌莱顿队获胜的赔率是6:1，这就意味着如果你赌一个荷兰盾，你将赢得六个荷兰盾。”他解释道。

第62页

我笑了。“哦，真的吗？”我说。有时，最好让人们相信你什么也不懂。

“找到了，”他突然说，“这里有一些东西你可能会感兴趣。赌莱顿队获胜的大赌注，有三个50万荷兰盾的赌注。”那差不多是20万英镑。

我转过身去看电脑屏幕。这些赌注是一个博彩集团或组织下的，没有出现人名。下注的地点分别是阿姆斯特丹、莱顿和鹿特丹。这个集团的名字是“阿姆斯特丹联盟”。

这个名字对于我没有任何意义。

“哇！”我说，“150万荷兰盾……总计超过50万英镑……这是很大的赌注。这很平常吗？”

“嗯，”罗尼说，“不太常见，但确实有，而且这样做是允许的。我们从不问问题——这不是我们的工作。”

阿姆斯特丹联盟可能很高兴没人问问题。以6:1的赔率，他们赚了大约 300 万英镑。对于一晚上的工作而言业绩不差。

第63页

我向罗尼要了一份阿姆斯特丹联盟过去一年所下赌注的清单。他说他需要一天时间。我说我明天一大早再来。

“哦，还有今天晚上的比赛，我想知道是否有人在巴塞罗那队下了大赌注。”我离开时说。

我回到酒店，躺在床上思考。我打开电视，里面正在播放一场足球比赛。我不知道是哪两个队在打比赛，但是我看了一会儿。一个黄头发的前锋得到了球，他越过三个人射门。守门员扑向右边救球，但是没成功。黄头发小伙子进了一个漂亮的球，高兴得又蹦又跳。

那个守门员……我思量着。我关掉电视，暗笑起来。

第 10 章　一个警察

第64页

“你凭什么认为这个博彩集团，阿姆斯特丹联盟，与克里斯蒂亚安斯先生有关系呢？”德弗里斯问道。

我正和乔普·德弗里斯督察在位于伊兰运河岸边的警察总部谈话，他是阿姆斯特丹警察局刑侦队队长。我决定看看我们能否合作。但是他身材高大，面无笑容，而且和他交流很不容易——我明白为什么埃莉不喜欢他了。

“这是我的猜测，”我说，“但是我认为值得调查一下。”

德弗里斯盯着我。他不是一个喜欢猜测的人。我看得出我没有取得任何进展。而且坐在他的办公室里也令人不愉快。屋子里烟雾缭绕，他的办公桌上凌乱不堪。

“然后还有我在德派普遇见的那个家伙……”我说。

“那个家伙？”德弗里斯问道，又点燃了一支烟放到嘴里。

“是的。我不能告诉你他的名字，但是……”

“詹森小姐，”德弗里斯尽力耐心地说，“我怎么能相信一个我不知道名字的人说的话呢？”

第65页

我们俩都沉默了一会儿。我想马上离开，但又决定再多待一会儿。

“但是他说马克斯·卡森到德派普时就已经死了，”我说，“而你们抓到的那个人，那个叫沙普的家伙——只是偷了他的钱包。”

德弗里斯没说话。

“之后，我就在酒店外面的街道上遭到了袭击，”我说，“有人想吓唬我。”

我确信，无论是谁袭击了我，他们都是想阻止我找到真相。

“詹森小姐，对此我感到非常抱歉，”德弗里斯说，“阿姆斯特丹是一座非常安全的城市，但是这样的事情确实会发生。”

我不知道怎样才能让这个人明白。

“证据呢？”他继续说道，隔着桌子吹出一缕烟，直扑到我的脸上。“你的证据呢？你所掌握的只是一个人编的故事，而这个人几乎可以肯定是个罪犯。”

“我还没有任何证据，这是我的问题。”我冷静地说。“无论如何，我不是警察，督察，我是个新闻记者。你们才是应该找到证据的人。”我提醒他。

第66页

这是个错误。德弗里斯不是那种喜欢别人告诉他应该怎么做的人。“听着，詹森小姐，”他突然坐直身子说，“我建议你做好你自己的工作，我也会做好我的工作。我们这里的工作是讲究证据的。正如你所说，你不是警察。或许你最好别插手这件事。”他又补充道：“你们这些人只会增加我们工作的难度。”

荷兰的警察和英国的警察一样，我想，他们总是抱怨记者。

“听我说，督察，”我努力保持冷静地说道，“我是来给你们提供一些信息的，这对我没有任何好处。我只是想你们可能会调查一下。”

我起身离开。我觉得我是在对牛弹琴，浪费了很多时间。我必须要弄到一些证据。我走了，留下德弗里斯独自坐在他那烟雾缭绕的办公室里，坐在凌乱的办公桌旁。我要去看一场足球比赛。

第 11 章　一场足球比赛

第67页

“鹿特丹队的守门员是谁？”我们开着乔斯·范埃森的白色保时捷去鹿特丹时，我问他。

“劳尔·桑切斯，”他说，“怎么了？”

“跟我说说他吧。”我说。

“他是个很棒的守门员，是个好人。”乔斯说。

“不，我是说……他的家庭情况什么的。”我说。

“哦，好的。他来自哥伦比亚，他家很穷。我想卡森学校发现他时，他还是个八九岁的孩子。他当时正在波哥大的街上干活儿。”乔斯说着，将车子开上了去往鹿特丹的高速公路。

“卡森学校安排他们全家来了荷兰，是吗？”我问。

“不，不是这样。他们还生活在那里，但是现在劳尔有足够的钱让他们生活得舒适自在。”

对于一个年轻人来说，这是一个很大的责任，我想。劳尔·桑切斯必须确保他的家人一切都好。

自从在电视上看了那场足球比赛后，我一直在想守门员的事情。对于比赛的输赢，前锋固然非常重要，但是守门员同样也很重要。如果你想让一个球队输掉比赛，守门员就是最佳人选。

第68页

在驶往鹿特丹的路上，我和乔斯聊了各种各样的事情。乔斯把他将来的打算告诉了我。或许他会去英国管理一支足球队，在那里开始新的生活。他已经收到了一些大型俱乐部的邀约。

大约6:50我们来到了鹿特丹足球俱乐部。我们把车停在停车场，朝体育场走去。

“我们必须快点儿，”乔斯说，“否则我们会错过比赛的开局。”

我们进入拥挤的体育场，找到了我们的座位。作为一名退役球员，乔斯能搞到最好位置的票。我环顾四周，来观看比赛的大概有五万人。比赛双方的球迷们又唱又喊，喧闹声很大。

我们坐好后不到一分钟，裁判员吹了哨，比赛开始了。鹿特丹队上半场踢得非常好，进了第一个球。他们的明星前锋里特，飞起最擅长的左脚射门得分，球从球门的一角飞了进去。巴塞罗那队的守门员想去扑球，但是没有够到。上半场结束时鹿特丹队1:0领先。鹿特丹队的球迷们尖叫着，狂喊着。

第69页

在下半场，巴塞罗那队踢得更好一些，尽管有一段时间无人射门。之后，比赛大约进行到 75 分钟时，他们的优秀前锋马丁内兹终于发起了进攻，他绕过一个、两个、三个人。巴塞罗那队的球迷们开始尖叫：“马丁内兹！马丁内兹！”马丁内兹冲到了球门前。他把球射进了球门的右上角。鹿特丹队的守门员桑切斯向球扑去，但是球从他的手指间穿过，进了球门。比分为 1∶1 平！巴塞罗那队的球迷们欣喜若狂。

接着，大约十分钟之后，马丁内兹再得一分。又一次，桑切斯碰到了球，但是球从他的手指间穿了过去。桑切斯表现得根本不好。巴塞罗那队的球迷们变得更疯狂了！随后，裁判吹响了终场哨声。巴塞罗那队 2∶1 获胜。

第70页

我们尽可能快地离开了体育场，尽量避开人群。“谢谢你。”乔斯发动车子准备开回阿姆斯特丹时我说，“比赛很精彩！”尽管鹿特丹队输了，但是比赛依然很激动人心。自从多年前马克斯带我去看了曼联的比赛之后，我就再也没去看过球赛。

第71页

乔斯看起来不是很高兴。“巴塞罗那队是一只了不起的球队，但是鹿特丹队本应该获胜的。好了，但愿和阿贾克斯队的比赛他们能踢得好一些。”

“他们什么时候和阿贾克斯比赛？”我问。阿贾克斯是来自阿姆斯特丹的球队。

“星期六，”乔斯回答，“只有三天了。这是一场重大的比赛，获胜对于鹿特丹队来说很重要。”

我们开车返回阿姆斯特丹，一路上都在谈论这场球赛。

终于我们到了洲际酒店。当车停在酒店外面时，乔斯说：“哦，我有东西要送给你，凯特。”

他从后座上拿起一个棕色的大信封，里面是一张照片的复印件，是我在乔斯位于欧德斯堡的公寓里见过的那张——鹿特丹队的照片。

“我看到你喜欢这张照片，”他笑着说，“所以送你一张。”他把照片递给我。

“噢，谢谢，”我说，“你真是太好了，乔斯。你可以在背面签上你的名字，可能的话再写几句话吗？”

第72页

“当然可以。”乔斯从口袋里拿出一支笔，把照片翻过来。“你想让我写什么？”

“‘赠给我的朋友，凯特’怎么样？”我建议。

“我亲爱的朋友。”乔斯笑着说。

他写完之后，又把照片放进信封，递给了我。“晚安，凯特。”他说。

我下了车，看着他开车离去。然后我把照片从信封里拿出来，低头看了看。上面写着：“赠给我亲爱的朋友（注：原文用的是错误拼写 freind，凯特由此确认当初给她寄信的人就是乔斯）凯特，爱你的乔斯。”

我的脑子飞快地转动着。看来乔斯就是我的那位“朋友”。他知道，或者自以为知道发生了什么事情。我只是希望他提供的信息比他的拼写更准确。

我沉思着走进酒店。我得和乔斯谈一谈。我决定第二天去见他。

可是对于乔斯·范埃森来说再也没有第二天了。那天夜里，他被发现死在了他位于欧德斯堡的公寓外面。

第 12 章　守门员

第73页

“我们从阿姆斯特丹联盟说起吧。”我对劳尔·桑切斯这个鹿特丹城市足球俱乐部的守门员说。

“什么？”他问。

桑切斯是一个很帅气的男人，有着深棕色的皮肤和一头黑色卷发。他那双棕色的眼睛看起来很惊讶，但是我有一种感觉，他完全知道我在说什么。不过我进行了解释，只是想确认一下。

“阿姆斯特丹联盟，”我解释说，“是一个财团的名字，他们把一大笔钱赌在与鹿特丹城市足球俱乐部比赛的球队上。他们赚了几百万。”

我在桑切斯位于阿姆斯特丹城外的房子里和他交谈。那天是星期五。就在前一天，乔斯·范埃森被发现在自己的公寓外被刺身亡。他的钱包不见了。又一次，谋杀者看起来像抢劫。我很生气，想知道答案。

“我不知道你在说什么，詹森小姐，”桑切斯说，“我想你最好离开这里。”他站了起来。

第74页

“坐下，”我说，“在搞清楚发生了什么事情之前，我哪儿也不去。”

守门员坐下了。

“听着，劳尔，听好了，”我继续严肃地说，“我的两个朋友死了，我很生气，非常生气。我知道有人在下很大的赌注，赌鹿特丹队输。”

“那又怎么样呢?”他问。

“我知道你是一名非常优秀的守门员，但你昨天晚上的表现就像个五岁的小孩子。我也知道，”为了让他明白，我又补充道，“如果我把我知道的告诉警察，而你又不帮助他们，你就会蹲很长时间的监狱。我会告诉警察的。你会失去你的足球生涯，你的家人会重新过穷苦日子。你自己选吧。”

我看着他。他坐在那儿，低着头看着双脚。他沉默了半天，不过最终我看到我的话开始起作用了。也许是乔斯·范埃森的死让这位鹿特丹队的守门员明白他在玩一场很危险的游戏。

“好吧，是的……”桑切斯深吸一口气说道，“有人给了我一大笔钱，你知道的，让我输掉比赛。”

第75页

桑切斯看起来很不高兴。

“有人要求你输掉比赛?”我重复道。

我知道这种事在足球比赛或其他运动中时有发生。大约两年前，英国也曾经发生过一起重大案件，伦敦的一家俱乐部参与其中。犯罪分子给著名球员钱让他们输掉比赛：如果他们是前锋，则射门不中；如果他们是守门员，则救球不力。然后犯罪分子下大赌注赌另一支球队获胜。在他们被抓之前，他们用这种方式已经赚了数百万英镑。当然，球员也被送进了监狱。

“是的，”桑切斯轻声说，“但是……”

“但是你不想干了，对吗?”我问。

守门员点点头。

“是汤姆·卡森让你输掉比赛的吗？”我问。

“不，不，不是卡森先生。”他说。

“那是谁？”我问。

“克里斯蒂亚安斯，”他说，“马丁·克里斯蒂亚安斯。”我看着对面的桑切斯。他的脸几乎变白了——他是一个受到惊吓的人。

第76页

看来这就是克里斯蒂亚安斯在做的事情：接管俱乐部，为自己赚数百万，很可能有一些朋友在帮他。但是为什么汤姆·卡森会让他这样做？或许汤姆·卡森也害怕克里斯蒂亚安斯。但是为什么呢？

“汤姆知道克里斯蒂亚安斯的所作所为吗？”我问。

“是的，当然……嗯，他一定知道，”桑切斯说，“但是他没办法阻止他，我也说不准是为什么，但是他就是无能为力。”

“那你一开始为什么没有报警？”我说。

“我太害怕了。”桑切斯说。

“害怕？”我问。

“当然。”他说，看上去很担心，“我可能会失去一切。我有四个兄弟姐妹，他们将不得不辍学，重新流浪街头。我妈妈又会很穷了。”

可怜的桑切斯，他陷入了进退两难的境地。

“而且克里斯蒂亚安斯是一个危险人物，”他补充说，他那双棕色的眼睛睁得更大了，“我的意思是非常危险。你也看到马克斯和乔斯·范埃森的遭遇了。”

大家都很害怕的原因很明显。

“我很早就知道我必须停止这么干了，”这位鹿特丹队的守门员说，“我只是不知道该怎么做。”

第77页

“明天与阿贾克斯的比赛，”我说，“他们也要求你输了吗？”

“是的。”他轻声说。他的眼睛里再一次流露出恐惧。

“别担心，”我对桑切斯说，“我想我们可以做点儿什么。但是我们必须迅速行动，我们需要证据，一些让警察看的东西。”

又一次，我唯一的希望就是埃莉了。我打电话给她。

“埃莉，你听我说，”我说，“我又得让你帮忙了。”

“哦，我现在很忙，凯特，”她说，“一小时以后我能到那儿。”

我给了她桑切斯家的地址，然后放下了电话。

一小时之后，埃莉坐着看着我和桑切斯，认真听着。我把事情原原本本都告诉了她。从她的表情我能看得出她相信我。

“所以，埃莉，”我问，“你能给我们弄一台录音机和一个麦克风吗？你知道，就是那种能装在口袋里的，或类似的。”

我知道警察会使用微型麦克风和录音机，能藏在包里或口袋里，甚至别在人的衣服上。埃莉说她觉得能找到。

第78页

“埃莉，”我说，“还有一件事情。”

“什么？”她问。

“马克斯·卡森的心脏不好。乔斯告诉我他在吃药。我需要知道警察有没有在他的房间里或身上发现药，我需要知道瓶子里有多少药片、卖给他药的药剂师的名字以及买药的时间。”我说。

“就这些吗？”她问。

“是的，如果你能尽快得到这些信息……”我说着，奉上了我最甜美的笑容。

第 13 章 计划

第79页

一个小时之后，埃莉带着录音机和麦克风回来了。

“现在我说一下我要你做的事情，”我对劳尔说，“我们要把这个麦克风和录音机放在你的外套里。只要记得在克里斯蒂亚安斯说话时靠近他就行。”

然后劳尔给克里斯蒂亚安斯打了电话，约好到他家去见他。“我只是想谈点儿事情。”劳尔高兴地说。

当他到了克里斯蒂亚安斯家时，劳尔打算告诉他，他想要更多的钱作为表现糟糕的代价。我们都希望克里斯蒂亚安斯能开口说话，说一些他在做的事情，而劳尔会给他录音。对于劳尔来讲，这是非常危险的，但是如果成功了，这就能给我们提供所需要的证据。

“我和劳尔一起去吧，”埃莉说，“我在附近等着。”

和克里斯蒂亚安斯见过面之后，埃莉也能确保劳尔不受到伤害。她带了一条牛仔裤和一件短上衣，而且她现在已经换下了警服。

第80页

“噢，”我补充道，“药片查得如何了？有发现吗？”

“有，警方确实在马克斯的房间里发现了一些药片，”她说，“这些药叫作拉诺辛，是两周前从海牙的一个药剂师那里买的。一瓶有60片，每天只能吃一片。当他们发现这些药时，瓶子里大约还剩30片。”

拉诺辛……拉诺辛……我记得在哪儿听过这个名字，但是现在我想不起来了。

埃莉和劳尔走了。我该去坎特斯见罗尼了。

我打车来到了坎特斯的办公室。我到那儿时，罗尼正坐在他的电脑前，和我昨天见到的情形一模一样，就好像他从来没回过家。他把我所需要的信息用电脑打印出来了。

我看着打印出来的东西，内容非常有意思。正如我之前想的那样，信息显示，在过去的一年里，阿姆斯特丹联盟定期投注赌鹿特丹队输。还有一大笔赌注下在巴塞罗那队会打赢星期三的比赛。阿姆斯特丹联盟又故技重演了。然而，押在第二天鹿特丹与阿贾克斯的比赛上的钱要多得多。

第81页

我把电脑打印出来的东西放入一个信封里，把它寄到了我入住的酒店，信封上写着我的名字。这样，无论发生什么事，它明天都会寄到酒店。

我回到酒店等着埃莉和劳尔回来。我通过客房服务点了一些茶水等待着。我喝着茶。一个小时过去了，然后两个小时过去了。随着时间的流逝，我变得越来越担心。他们在哪儿？我们约好了只要他们拿到录有证据的磁带就回酒店碰面。我试着看书，然后看电视，但是都看不下去。我满脑子都是可怕的想法，不知道他们发生了什么。

我躺在床上，努力让自己放松。马克斯所服用的药片的名字又出现在我的脑海里。拉诺辛。是的！就是它！拉诺辛含有地高辛，是一种强效的心脏药物，如果服用过量可致命。我第一次听说拉诺辛是在伦敦的一次新闻报道中。一位医生用这种药杀害了他的妻子。这种药用来杀人再合适不过了，因为地高辛在体内 12 小时之后就找不到了。或许有人让马克斯超量服用了拉诺辛，用这种方式杀死了他！或许伯特终究是对的。或许马克斯在德派普被人刺杀之前就已经死了。

第82页

然后，终于，大约7:00，有人敲门。谢天谢地，我想。我跳起来开门，以为会看到埃莉和劳尔。突然，我被推回到房间内。一个穿着黑色西装的高个子男人快速进门，用手捂住了我的嘴。正是三天前在酒店外面袭击我的那个人，同样的黑发和清澈的蓝眼睛。

“克里斯蒂亚安斯？”我问。

“别出声！”他在我耳边说，“否则我就杀了你。”

我把这当成他承认了自己的身份。

第14章　被劫持

第83页

克里斯蒂亚安斯把我推到房间的另一侧。我看见他手里拿着枪。“东西在哪儿？”他说。

“什么在哪儿？”我问，努力保持冷静。

“打印的材料！”他说，“我刚才拜访了你的朋友罗尼，我想他不会再帮你了。现在告诉我打印的材料在哪儿？”

“埃莉和劳尔在哪里？你把他们怎么了？”我大喊。我很生气。

他露出了狰狞的笑容。“他们很好，”他说，“但是他们很愚蠢。劳尔应该清楚，不能和我作对。你的警察朋友不应该掺和她一无所知的事情。”

“他们在哪儿？”我又问。我想打他，但是他的枪口正对着我。

“他们非常安全。如果劳尔明天要为我们发挥出‘最好’或者我应该说‘最差’的状态的话，我们就需要他的身体好好的。”

“他永远不会那样做的。”我说。

“哦，我想他会的，”克里斯蒂亚安斯说着又笑了，“如果他想让你和埃莉活着的话。”

第84页

“你不会得逞的，”我说，“警察总部会发现埃莉失踪了。”

“明天是星期六，”他说，“谁会想她？等到有人想她或你时，比赛已经结束了。我将成为千万富翁，我早已远走高飞了。现在，”他继续说，表情也严肃起来，“你该和你的朋友们待在一起了。比赛结束之前，我需要你老老实实地别妨碍我。跟我来，我们到外面走一走。记住，这把枪正对着你。如果你发出一点儿声音，我就开枪打死你。”

在我们离开房间之前，他把枪藏在大衣底下，抵着我的后背。然后他把我推出了门，下了楼，从酒店的后门走了出去。他又高又壮，而且就站在身后用枪抵着我的后背，做任何尝试都是愚蠢的。在酒店外面，他把我推到一辆小型厢式货车的后面，车窗是黑色的。接着我就什么都不知道了。

* * *

我意识到的第一件事情是疼痛；非常疼，从后脑勺开始一直蔓延到眼睛。

第85页

起初，我仿佛置身于一片漆黑之中。后来我的眼睛适应了，我看见上方有一扇窗户透出一点儿光来。头疼让我很难思考，但是我猜自己是躺在一个房间里的地板上，位于一座房子下面，或许是个地窖。地板是石头铺的，坚硬、肮脏、寒冷。

我检查了我的身体。这很难，因为我被铐起来了——我的双手被铐在身体前面。坚硬的手铐划破了我的手。除了头疼得厉害，我似乎没什么问题。接着我的眼睛更加适应了黑暗，我环顾房间。在房间的一个角落里的是埃莉，她戴着手铐，嘴被堵上了，所以说不了话。她闭着双眼，但是我看到她在呼吸；她没有死，但是我想她失去知觉了。她的头在流血。我不知道劳尔在哪儿。

我必须迅速思考和行动。一旦比赛结束，克里斯蒂亚安斯拿到了钱，会发生什么事情？我明白，像克里斯蒂亚安斯这样的人，不可能放我们走。我非常确信，他无论如何都会杀了我们。也许他会让我们的死看起来像是毫无意义的刺杀，然后在深夜把我们的尸体扔到大街上。他就是这么对待马克斯和乔斯的。照他的说法来看，他显然订好了票，比赛一结束就飞去某个国家。或许他会把我们留在这个地窖里等死。

第86页

我来到埃莉面前，和她说话。开始时她一动不动，但是后来，慢慢地，她的眼睛睁开了一点儿。她看着我，好像不认识我似的。

“埃莉，听我说，”我低声说，“是我，凯特。我要想办法离开这儿，但是我很快会回来的，好吗？我会找人来帮忙的。”

她又闭上了眼睛。

我听到什么地方有说话的声音，我知道我没有多少时间了。我必须离开这里，而且也要想办法救出埃莉。这似乎不可能。

我又抬起头望着那扇窗户。对，我想，我们是在地窖里，那扇窗户很可能对着街道，也很可能有台阶通向街道。这些地窖在阿姆斯特丹很常见。窗户在我上方大约两米高的地方，而且很小。幸运的是窗户开了一道小缝隙，底下有一块石板。石板不是很宽，但是或许够用了。如果我能够到石板就好了！但是怎么才能够到呢？即使我能够到它，怎么才能钻过窗户？我很苗条，但是窗户看起来很小。

第87页

我慢慢走到有窗户的那面墙那里，用手背摸了摸。我慢慢地向上移动我的手，想尽力找个可以落脚的地方。什么都没有。

我向后退，离开窗户，朝房间的一个角落退去。当我在黑暗中移动时，差一点儿被身后的什么东西绊倒。是把椅子！椅子很破旧，似乎也不是很结实，但毕竟是把椅子。我开始小心地把它拉到小窗户下面。这是我唯一的希望。

要移动椅子而不发出声音是很难的。地板上的任何动作都会发出很大的声音，而金属手铐使我不能搬起椅子。我努力慢慢呼吸。过了很长时间，我终于把椅子挪到了窗户下。该试试了，看看它能否承受住我的体重。如果椅子不够结实，我摔了下来，楼上的人肯定会听到声响，来到地窖，那一切就全完了。

我先在椅子上坐了坐，没问题。然后我慢慢地、小心翼翼地踩了上去。令我惊讶的是，椅子没有断裂。我伸手去够窗户，并设法摸到了它。外面漆黑一片，我猜天一定很晚了。我一定昏迷了很长时间。

第88页

就在这时，我听到身后有一个很低的声音。我转过身来，是埃莉想说话。

“嘘！埃莉，”我低声说，“我很快就回来，我保证。”我说这话的时候，不知道自己说的是不是真的，不知道自己是否真能保证。

我转回身面对窗户。我感觉到了透过窗户进来的夜晚的空气，听到了汽车的声音，还有雨声。雨已经下了一阵了。或许我能从窗户爬出去，我想。我必须尽力把自己向上拉。如果我掉回到椅子上，将会发出很大的声音，那样的话，我们就都完了。

我伸出手，尽最大努力往上拉动身体。我慢慢地爬到了窗户下面的石板上。由于练过多年的空手道，我的胳膊非常强壮。我感到有新鲜空气扑面而来。我吸了一口气，给自己补充新的力量。我回头看了看埃莉。如果我能逃走，或许我能找人来帮忙。

我推开窗户，先伸出戴着手铐的双手，接着伸出头。我能看见距离地面只有一米，但是我能穿过这扇窄小的窗户吗？

第89页

我把膝盖顶在石板上，喘着粗气。最后用力一推，我就出来了！我双手按在地上，肩膀着地。我之前对台阶的猜测是正确的。我躺在大约十个石头台阶的底部。我迅速站起来，跑上台阶，来到大街上。我抬头看了看那座房子。我以前见过这座房子——是克里斯蒂亚安斯位于绅士运河岸边的住所。我奋力沿街跑着。现在雨下得很大。我一直跑个不停。

我一路跑到位于伊兰运河的中央警察局。当我跑进门时，坐在桌旁的年轻警察奇怪地看着我。我从头到脚都湿透了，还戴着手铐。他给我打开手铐时，我快速告诉他发生了什么事。“我们必须马上回到绅士运河，”我说，“不能耽搁！克里斯蒂亚安斯很危险！”

那个警察叫来了另外三名警察。我和其中两个人上了一辆车，另外两名警察跟着上了另外一辆车。当我们开车前往绅士运河时，我告诉了警察更多内幕。我告诉他们我不知道劳尔在哪儿，我很担心他。五分钟之后，我们把车停在了克里斯蒂亚安斯家的拐角处。

第90页

其中两名警察绕到那座房子的前面，另外两名跑到房子的后面。这样做的意图是当两名警察在前面按响门铃时，在后面的两名警察会把门踢开，救出埃莉。

我坐在车里，冷得发抖。那名警察之前给了我一条毯子，我把它裹在身上努力让自己暖和起来。我能看见房子后面的那两名警察。他们破门而入时发出一声巨响，然后是一片寂静。每一分钟慢得如同一个小时。突然我听到一声枪响！谁中枪了？“求你了，上帝，但愿不是埃莉。”我心里想。我留神听是不是有更多的枪声，但是什么也没听到。

终于，大约 15 分钟之后，两名警察押着克里斯蒂亚安斯从房子里走了出来。血从克里斯蒂亚安斯的腿上流下来。我向前坐了坐，希望很快就能看见埃莉。接着，几分钟之后，另外两名警察搀扶着埃莉出来了，她后面跟着劳尔！这么说他一直在房子里！他看上去还好。埃莉看起来很糟糕，但是她还活着。

第91页

其中一名警察帮助埃莉上了车坐在我旁边，劳尔从另一侧上了车。

“谢天谢地，你平安无事。”我说着抓住了埃莉的手。

第92页

她虚弱地朝我一笑。

“到底发生了什么？”我问他们。

“哦，一切都按计划进行，”劳尔说，“克里斯蒂亚安斯和我谈话，然后我带着磁带离开了他的房子。”

“是的，”埃莉说，“然后劳尔出来了，绕过街角来跟我会合。但是克里斯蒂亚安斯跟踪了他。他手里拿着枪，逼着我们返回他家。我想克里斯蒂亚安斯很狡猾。劳尔一打电话说要去见他，他很可能就意识到发生了什么事。”

“当我们回到房子里时，他把埃莉打晕了，把我锁进另外一间屋子里，”劳尔说，“他需要我参加比赛。而且他也需要埃莉——他告诉我如果我不参加比赛并输给阿贾克斯队，他就杀了她。”

很幸运，劳尔是克里斯蒂亚安斯计划中的重要人物。如果他不是，他和埃莉有可能已经被当场杀害了。

第 15 章　真相

第93页

凌晨 3:00，我和埃莉坐在德弗里斯烟雾缭绕的办公室里。她在警察局看过医生，感觉好些了。德弗里斯非常生气她把自己置于如此危险的境地，但主要还是为她平安无事而高兴。

劳尔把所有事实真相都告诉了德弗里斯，然后获准回了家。之后他将必须提供证据，但是他可能不会被判入狱。

我的头很痛，但我终于给了德弗里斯他所需要的证据，这些证据将会让克里斯蒂亚安斯在监狱里待上很长时间。

“马克斯·卡森不愿意玩克里斯蒂亚安斯的游戏。”我说，“马克斯发现了正在发生的事情，他试图阻止克里斯蒂亚安斯，但是没成功。我猜马克斯星期四晚上要去见的那个人就是克里斯蒂亚安斯，很可能是去告诉他收手或警告他自己要报警。克里斯蒂亚安斯不允许这样的事情发生，所以杀了他。”

“所以他在家里用刀刺死了马克斯？”德弗里斯问。

“不是的，”我回答，“我在德派普遇见的那个人说得没错，马克斯在被刀刺之前就死了。不知怎么的，克里斯蒂亚安斯让马克斯服用了过量的拉诺辛，马克斯治心脏病的药。或许他把药放在了酒中。”

第94页

我给他讲了地高辛，告诉他这种药服用 12 小时之后在体内就找不到痕迹了。“马克斯的药瓶里少了很多片药。”我说。

“但是后来为什么用刀捅他呢？”德弗里斯问。

“这个嘛，不管怎样，克里斯蒂亚安斯需要处理掉一具尸体，”我解释道，“他不想把尸体就那样扔到大街上，因为警方会调查马克斯的死因。你们很可能会立即做尸检，从而发现马克斯体内残留的药物。克里斯蒂亚安斯觉得，让你们认为马克斯是被街头罪犯用刀捅死的会更加安全。”

“他的办法差一点儿就成功了，”埃莉说，“做尸检的时候，我们没能发现药物。”

德弗里斯看着我。“那么，范埃森呢？”他问。

“嗯，很不幸，他知道得太多了，”我说，“他拒绝拿克里斯蒂亚安斯的钱，并试图置身事外。他甚至离开了他热爱的足球俱乐部。我想他看到足球界所发生的事情很伤心。他有他的梦想……”

“但是若要忘掉此事太难了，”我继续说，“他喜欢马克斯，而且知道他的处境艰难。之后马克斯被杀，乔斯确信此事是克里斯蒂亚安斯所为……再后来，我来了。”我停了下来。我不知道如果我不来阿姆斯特丹，如果我没有让乔斯·范埃森再次参与其中，他是否还会活着。我突然感到很难过。

第95页

“而且，”我补充道，“明天邮件寄来时，你就能看到阿姆斯特丹联盟的证据了——我指的是今天！”

克里斯蒂亚安斯很有可能毁掉了坎特斯博彩局电脑上的证据，但是至少还有一份纸质副本。然后我想起了罗尼。他遭遇了什么事情呢？

“他没事，”德弗里斯说，“克里斯蒂亚安斯稍微打伤了他，并严重威胁了他，但是没有杀他。”

“那阿姆斯特丹联盟的其他成员呢？”我问。我猜克里斯蒂亚安斯有三四位‘朋友’是这个集团的成员。

德弗里斯笑了。“我们现在正找他们呢，詹森小姐。”他说。

“还有一件事我不太明白，”埃莉说，“为什么汤姆·卡森允许克里斯蒂亚安斯收购他的俱乐部呢？”

第96页

“对啊，”我说，“我也想知道。”

“那我们为什么不问问他呢？”德弗里斯说，“他在隔壁的审讯室。我把他带过来。”德弗里斯起身离开了房间。

我和埃莉看了一眼彼此。我的头还在疼，但是我想和他谈谈，我必须和他谈谈。不久，德弗里斯回来了，汤姆·卡森跟在他身后。见到我，汤姆看起来很开心。他比我上次见到他的时候快乐多了。

“詹森小姐，”他说，“我真高兴这一切都结束了。”他笑得很灿烂，在我们对面的桌旁坐了下来。

“但是你为什么让克里斯蒂亚安斯接管俱乐部呢？”我问，“我不明白。”

“我别无选择，”卡森说，“俱乐部经营得不是很好。我们在八十年代末、九十年代初表现很好，之后我们开始走下坡路。我们失去了一些最优秀的球员。我们需要钱来买新球员，真正优秀的球员，而且还要重建体育场。”

我记得我之前见过的体育场很新——也很漂亮。

“我们四处求援，但是没有人愿意给俱乐部投资。后来克里斯蒂亚安斯出现了，”卡森继续说，“他主动给我们俱乐部提供大笔资金。但是当然，他想要股份，一开始是 10%。”

第97页

卡森深吸了一口气。“俱乐部是我生命的全部，”他说，“我是 20 年前创办的这个俱乐部，在我退役几年之后。你要知道，拥有一家足球俱乐部和一所足球学校是我的梦想……真正为荷兰足球做点儿什么。我不能让鹿特丹城市足球俱乐部就这样消失。我太热爱它了。”

汤姆·卡森又深吸了一口气。

“所以，”他继续说，“起初一切都正常。但是不久克里斯蒂亚安斯开始要求得到更多股份。然后事情就发生了……但是很长一段时间内，我都不知道克里斯蒂亚安斯到底在做什么。”

“你是什么时候发现阿姆斯特丹联盟的？”我问道。

“大约一年前，”他说，“但是那时克里斯蒂亚安斯已经拥有了俱乐部 45% 的股份，他处于强势地位。他说如果我去报警，他就告诉警察我也是这个联盟的一员。克里斯蒂亚安斯说警方永远不会相信我对此事一无所知。我还以为马克斯会有办法……他总是能想到办法。”

第98页

汤姆 · 卡森苦笑了一下。克里斯蒂亚安斯太强大了，即使对马克斯来说。

“嗯……剩下的事情你都知道了，”汤姆说，“马克斯认为我们应该报警，但是我拿不定主意。我们为这事争吵过。我不想去报警，因为我知道克里斯蒂亚安斯是多么危险。我为自己和球员们担惊受怕。”

“你现在想怎么办？”我问。

“回到俱乐部，努力让它真正运转起来。”他笑着说。

我握着汤姆的手说：“祝你好运，汤姆，我相信你一定能行。”

我累了，起身要走。

“詹森小姐，”德弗里斯说，他终于笑了，而且伸出了手，“谢谢。”

我也朝他笑笑。这位督察不是一个好相处的人，但是他知道自己错了。虽然我对德弗里斯微笑，但是我并不觉得很高兴。我本想给他证据，向他证明我是对的，但是现在我在这里了，一切似乎没那么重要了。我满脑子想的都是马克斯和乔斯。他们死了，没有什么能使他们死而复生。

第 16 章　再见，阿姆斯特丹

第99页

我打开德弗里斯办公室的门。我一晚上没睡觉，现在开始有点儿困了。埃莉跟着我出来了。

“你要回酒店吗？”她问。

“是的，”我说，“如果我还想要伦敦的那份工作的话，我必须写一篇报道。”我朝她笑笑补充说：“哦，埃莉，谢谢你所做的一切。你是一个真正的朋友。”

她伸出双臂搂住我。“是啊，也谢谢你，凯特。”埃莉说，“还有，凯特……”

“嗯？”

“暂时别来阿姆斯特丹了，好吗？我觉得我承受不了了。”她大笑着说。

我吻了埃莉，然后离开了警察局。我穿过城里空荡荡的街道走回酒店。它们现在对我来说是安全的，因为克里斯蒂亚安斯被关进了牢房。海水的咸味使我头脑清醒了，早晨的阳光在运河的水面上闪烁。阿姆斯特丹又变得美丽动人起来。

第100页

我边往回走边想起了那些留在阿姆斯特丹的人：埃莉，她为了帮我将自己置身于极大的危险之中；劳尔，他最终鼓起勇气做了正确的事情；我可怜的“朋友”乔斯，他失去了生命；汤姆·卡森失去了哥哥。我看着运河黑暗的河水，想起了马克斯。多年前，马克斯救了我一命。他在我需要的时候为我而战。当他不能为自己而战的时候，我必须为他而战。或许这就是友谊的意义，或许是唯一正确的意义。

我开始写新闻稿件。一小时之后，上午8:30，我终于写完了。我把它传真回伦敦的办公室。当巴尔扎诺上班时，稿件就已经到了。

我躺在床上，筋疲力尽，睡着了。电话把我吵醒了，是巴尔扎诺打来的，他大声喊着，但是这一次他很高兴：“很棒的报道，詹森！”

“谢谢。”我说，“对了，戴夫，我想请两周假。我需要休个假。”

我把电话从耳边拿开，笑了。有些事情永远不会改变。